DEMON HAUNTED

TRUE STORIES FROM THE JOHN ZAFFIS VAULT

DEMON HAUNTED

TRUE STORIES FROM THE JOHN ZAFFIS VAULT

John Zaffis and Rosemary Ellen Guiley

Visionary Living, Inc.
New Milford, Connecticut

Demon Haunted: True Stories from the John Zaffis Vault

By John Zaffis and Rosemary Ellen Guiley

Cover design by Dan LeRoy
Interior design by Leslie McAllister

ISBN: 978-1-942157-06-9 (pbk)
ISBN: 978-1-942157-07-6 (e-book)

Published by Visionary Living, Inc.
New Milford, Connecticut
www.visionaryliving.com

Table of Contents

Foreword by Paul Eno   vii
Introduction by Rosemary Ellen Guiley   ix

1. Mirror Head   1

2. Demonic Images   15

3. Demon Haunted Things and Places   29

4. Relics of Painful Deaths   41

5. The Demon Box   51

6. Foul Things in Containers   61

7. The Burned Altar   75

8. Corrupted Religious Objects   85

9. The Thing in the Stone Egg   93

10. The Enchanted Walking Stick   99

11. Hudson Valley Havoc   107

12. A Spirited Liquor Cabinet   125

13. The Mystery of Walkabout Objects   133

14. Messages from Ed Warren   161

Resources   191
About the Authors   193

Foreword
By Paul Eno

I first met John Zaffis at the home of his uncle and aunt, Ed and Lorraine Warren, in the mid-1970s. Two years my junior, he was friendly but didn't say much. Now John is front and center, carrying the Warrens' ideas and methods well into a new century through books, television, film and lectures.

I first encountered Rosemary Ellen Guiley through several of her countless books, in the early 1990s. Her encyclopedic knowledge of paranormal history and tradition are astounding. Whenever Rosemary appears as a guest or guest co-host on our Boston/Providence radio show, *Behind the Paranormal with Paul & Ben Eno,* we aptly dub her the "Paranormal Renaissance Woman."

Now these two legendary researchers once again combine their considerable experience and talents to give us *Demon Haunted: True Stories from the John Zaffis Vault,* with jarring cases of negative entities and echoes of tragedy from John's own files. Ranging from strange items bought by collectors who got more than they bargained for, to artifacts from the terrible trauma of the 9/11 attacks, you are in for a fascinating tour of the bizarre.

While there can be debate on just what the paranormal is all about, there is no doubt that negative entities exist, that they are hungry and hostile, and that they can somehow be bound to objects. Much the same applies to tragic events. This book will give you an eyeful.

From another viewpoint, as a professional editor for nearly thirty-five years, I must compliment the authors for an excellently written tome. I find that the stories carry me along with their easy, conversational style, not failing to fully inform along the way.

So buckle up, open your mind and enjoy! It could happen to you.

Introduction
By Rosemary Ellen Guiley

Is it more frightening to see something you cannot explain, or to hear it and feel it around you, unseen, its appearance left totally to your wildly racing imagination? What if you feel "it" is *inside* of you?

To be "demon haunted" is an experience you will never forget.

Earth is a haunted planet. Throughout history, human beings have had daily contact with otherworldly residents and visitors whose actions range from benign to aggressive, and from mischievous to deadly. Humans have described, explained, catalogued, summoned, and exorcized these interlopers for centuries.

Even a mere half century ago, the landscape of the paranormal looked vastly different than it does today, thanks to advances in technology and parapsychology research, an increase in paranormal investigation, and a greater understanding of the energies of the land and the powers of human consciousness. "Hauntings" once were mostly attributed to the ghosts of the dead, or perhaps noisy spirits called poltergeists. Demonic possession cases were seldom in the public eye.

Today, we know that "the paranormal" is far more complex and cannot be explained simply. From quantum physics, we have the concept of "many worlds," multi-dimensional realities stacked next to each other, all of which might feature their own inhabitants. Our paranormal experiences demonstrate that doorways or portals exist both on the land and in human consciousness, which open up to these interdimensional realities in ways that awe us or terrify us, or both.

Our attention to the paranormal, through personal interest and involvement, and also the popular media, has increased our experiences. Some of those experiences are benign, even benevolent— and many of them are disturbing and problematic. "Demon haunted" cases are on the rise.

What do we mean by "demon haunted?"

In the ancient world, the demonic realm was viewed much differently than it is in the modern West. "Demons" included a wide range of spirits, from tricky to evil, meddlers who created a host of problems for people, including all the bad luck and ills of the world. They included low-level irritating beings and dangerous powerhouses who wielded the ability to destroy.

These beings and spirits are still round us—they never went away, because they exist alongside of us in interdimensional space. They continue to pose problems, shape-shifting in forms and tactics as humans have changed throughout the centuries.

Our backgrounds

John Zaffis has devoted more than forty years to working in the paranormal field, with an expertise in demonology and the "demon haunted." Among the thousands of cases he has handled are situations involving full possession by evil demons, and attached or haunted objects inhabited by spirits who act out aggressively against people. He has assisted in more than ninety cases of full demonic possession. He has dealt with cases of haunted land as well.

John's interest in the paranormal began early in life, and he had paranormal experiences—including an apparitional visit by his deceased grandfather—that added momentum to his quest to understand the supernatural realms that penetrate the physical world. He was fortunate to study under two of the biggest personalities in the modern demonology field, Ed and Lorraine Warren. Ed, who passed in 2006, was his blood uncle, the twin brother of his mother. Ed treated John like a son and mentored him, continuing his help after John launched his own successful career. In 1998, John founded the Paranormal Research Society of New England (PRSNE) and formed his own investigation teams.

One of John's special areas of expertise is haunted objects, things that have residues and attachments that create unpleasant and problematic phenomena. Many of the culprits come from the demonic realm, and also the human dead who are angry or unhappy. Over the years, John has collected thousands of afflicted articles given to him in his cases by victims who no longer want the items around.

These items are now officially John's Museum of the Paranormal, housed in a barn on his private property. It is John's goal to establish a public museum where many of these objects can be put on display, and where classes and workshops can be given to educate the public about the paranormal.

John's knowledge of haunted objects led to his hit reality television show on The Syfy Channel, *Haunted Collector*, which ran for three seasons, and then was picked up for reprise by Destination America.

Over the years, John has become one of the best-loved figures in the paranormal field, and has well earned the title of "Godfather of the Paranormal."

My own career in the paranormal spans more than thirty years of research and investigation. Like John, I became interested in the unseen realms at an early age. My work has spanned the paranormal, ufology, cryptozoology, and metaphysics, which are all interrelated in human encounters with the unknown. I've done ground-breaking research on the Djinn, entities who are often demon-like in behavior and who figure in many cases, but who are little-known in the West.

Early in my career, I saw the influences of the energy of the land, as well as the role of human consciousness, in many cases of hauntings, attachments, and even possession.

The books
In our first book, *Haunted by the Things You Love* (2014), we presented a selection of afflicted objects from John's cases that demonstrated a range of spirit activity, and also a range of causes: residual attachments, curses, earthbound energy, and occult summonings. We also discussed in depth the causes and players, warning signs, and remedies.

In *Demon Haunted: True Stories from the John Zaffis Vault*, we expand that horizon with a wider variety of cases, some of which involved both of us. Anything can become haunted, even "demon haunted," as demonstrated by the cases. Personal objects, possessions, clothing, art objects, jewelry, and even religious objects can all become haunted vehicles. The land can be haunted as well.

We discuss these cases from a broad and more complex perspective of objects + spirits + the dead + the land + consciousness of the living. Sometimes the cases resolved quickly, but in others there were no simple answers or solutions. "Demon haunted" has many angles.

We also discuss the players and causes of problems, and how solutions are applied. We have increased the amount of tutorial material.

With a few exceptions, real names are not used in order to protect the privacy of the individuals. We have also disguised other personal details for reasons of privacy, and we have recreated dialogue.

We thank everyone who contributed their experiences to this book.

Personal revelations from John

In addition to all of this exciting new material, *Demon Haunted* features a tremendous and rare exclusive: deeply personal material from John that he has never discussed widely in public before. Since the passing of Ed Warren in 2006, Ed has been reaching out to John from the Other Side with mysterious messages. These communications have been delivered through friends, mediums, technology (such as ghost boxes and real-time communication apps used in paranormal investigation), and even dreams. The messages have increased in frequency and urgency since John suffered a heart attack in 2015. A mystery is afoot. Now you, the reader, have been invited to share in the mystery, the final chapter of which has yet to be written!

1

Mirror Head

Mirror Head sat glittering and brooding in the window of a second hand antiques and odd finds shop, waiting for a new owner. Or victim. It was one and the same.

Mirror Head was made of a severed mannequin's bald head, and took its name from its skin of mirror shards. Dozens of sharp irregular pieces of mirrors were glued in a mosaic over the front of its head. The mosaic stretched down like a Mardi Gras mask over the bridge of the nose, ending at mid-cheek, leaving the lower face exposed. The face had been painted coal black. The eye sockets, black where eyes should be, gazed out beyond the physical world into the unseen realms. Mirror Head saw spirits—and the spirits looked back.

Someone, perhaps its maker, had given the head a necklace of semi-precious stones and glass beads wrapped in silver wire, which laid on the truncated neck. The top of the head carried a band of more semi-precious stones wrapped in silver wire. A prominent quartz crystal was stuck to the top of the head. It looked like a beacon. What was the beacon calling in?

People who walked by on the sidewalk always gawked at Mirror Head. It was so unusual. Some stared, some laughed and pointed and made rude jokes, some glanced and fled in horror. People who lived in town and had to pass the shop often always hurried by, averting their eyes. Mirror Head took it all in.

Waiting... waiting... waiting... for another owner victim to come along. The soulless eyes looked beyond time. Mirror Head was waiting, and it had all the time in the world.

And its time was now. Coming within range of the radar of it sightless eyes was a couple, a man and woman in their mid-forties. The woman had a mop of long brown hair that was blowing over her shoulders in the breeze. The man had dark hair, slightly wavy, in a receding hairline. They were laden with shopping bags, laughing and talking. Tourists.

The second the woman's gaze fell on Mirror Head. She stopped short, grabbing the arm of the man. Her red lipstick mouth fell open. Her voice came through the window glass.

"Ed, what the heck is *that*?"

The man studied Mirror Head.

The head felt a joke coming on.

The man shrugged. "I dunno—somebody flunked art class?" He smirked but the woman did not share his humor. He started to move on, but the woman held him back.

"Wait a minute, Ed." She peered through the window, eyeing the contents of the shop. She looked up at sign bearing the shop's name. "Let's go in," she said. "The place looks interesting."

The man sighed. "Jesus, Amy. How many estate shops do we have to hit? You've already bought out this burg."

The woman tugged on his sleeve, moving toward the door.

Outside, Mirror Head remained impassive, expressionless, the dark eyes looking afar. Inside, Mirror Head smiled. Contact.

"I wish I could give you an exotic history, but we don't know much about it," said the woman behind the counter. She had fetched Mirror Head out of the window, and rested it on the glass display case, next to the cash register. She adjusted her wire-rimmed glasses and smoothed her short gray hair. She put her bony, thin hands lightly around the base of the neck and kept her eyes downcast as she spoke. "The person who brought it in said she had gotten it out on the Coast. I

don't know if she bought it, or it was a gift." She cleared her throat. "It's...
quite unique. Handmade, but there is no artist signature. Definitely a
conversation piece."

Amy reached out and touched the head, running her fingers
over the mirror shards. Some of them felt sharp.

Mirror Head glittered, and it seemed to Amy that a glow spilled
out around it.

She felt a large hole at the back of the head and turned it around.
"Why, look at this—it's hollow." The back of the head was open, sliced in
half with surgical precision. She bent down and peered in. "What are all
these things inside?"

Small quartz crystals were wrapped into a wad and fixed to the
interior. The front of the opening bore a small mosaic of mirror shards,
as though the interior replicated the exterior.

"What is the purpose of this stuff?" Amy asked the shopkeeper.

The woman pursed her lips, still averting her gaze. "Your guess is
as good as mine."

A crucifix dangled from the tangle of silver wires entwined
around the back of the head. A quick chill ran through Amy, but she
shrugged it off.

"Why does it have a crucifix?"

"To keep the devil away," Ed said, sarcasm in his voice.

The shopkeeper kept a poker face and shrugged. "We have no
information on how or why it was made that way." She paused. "I would
think it's something artistic."

Amy turned the head back around and looked into the empty
black eyes. The head was mesmerizing, even though a current of dark
foreboding rolled beneath the surface of its strange appeal.

Amy's mind worked rapidly. She mentally scanned their house
for a suitable location for the head. It would have to be well displayed
somewhere. A showpiece. Something for their friends and guests to talk
about. An odd thought crossed her mind that people might be able to
talk to the head—and get a response.

"I love it," Amy announced. "I've never seen anything like it.
Let's get it."

Ed upended the head and saw the price sticker. He frowned.
"Good lord," he said to the shopkeeper. "You want this much for a
mannequin head with broken mirrors stuck on it?"

The shop, which had been warm against the fall weather outside, was suddenly chilly.

The shopkeeper looked at the price sticker. "Oh, well," she said, flustered. "I'm sure we can do better than that. It has been here a while." She named a price far below the sticker.

Ed raised his eyebrows in surprise. "What's wrong with it?"

"Nothing." The woman now appeared nervous. "Why, nothing at all." She gestured toward the window. "We could use the space. We have so many things in the back, you see..." her voice trailed off.

"Ed, let's not give her a hard time," Amy said. "Let's get it."

"But what are we going to do with it?"

Amy smiled. "I have just the place for it."

Inside, Mirror Head smiled.

The shopkeeper carefully wrapped the head in tissue paper and bubble wrap, and fetched a box for it to rest in. They all said their mutual thank you's and Amy and Ed departed, Ed cradling the head.

They stood outside the shop for a few minutes, quibbling about the head. Ed thought it unnecessary at any price. Amy placed it on a par with an art treasure.

As they turned to leave, movement inside the shop caught Amy's eye. Glancing in, she was startled to see the shopkeeper at the spot in the window that had been occupied by the head. She held a lighted bundle of sage in one hand, and was waving it back and forth across the empty spot. Her lips were moving. Amy had the distinct impression she was reciting a prayer.

Many superstitions exist about mirrors. It is said that breaking a mirror brings seven years of bad luck, and may even break the soul of the person who breaks the mirror. In ancient Rome, a culture rife with superstitious beliefs and magical practices, breaking a mirror meant the breaking of one's health for seven years. In some cultures, breaking a mirror meant someone in the family would die within a year.

What happens, then, to the person who smashes one or more mirrors to smithereens—and mounts them on an artificial head? And what happens to the person who acquires the head with broken pieces? Does the bad luck pass on? Amy and Ed were about to find out.

Once back home, Amy made settling Mirror Head a priority. The living room had the perfect wall for showcasing it. She moved accent tables around and relocated some items. She placed Mirror Head on a console table centered on the expanse of wall. As she handled the head, she noticed that it felt oddly cold, as though it had been stored in a refrigerated room. The house was always kept plenty warm in cool weather. There was no explanation for the coldness of the head. Amy, intent on her redecorating, passed it off.

Stepping back, she examined her handiwork. The head looked like it needed something else. She retrieved a large mirror in a black lacquer decorator frame and hung it over the head. She placed a few potted plants on either side of the head. On the opposite wall was another mirror that looked straight at the head and into the other mirror. From any angle in the room, one could see different views of the head in the mirrors, and sometimes multiple reflections that went back and forth.

What an effect! Perfect.

"Mom, that's gross." The voice of Amy and Ed's older daughter, Carolyn, seventeen, interrupted Amy's concentration.

"Seriously," Carolyn said, coming up behind Amy. "Gross."

Amy smiled. "Hello, sweetheart. I didn't hear you come in. I thought you were staying after school."

Carolyn heaved her shoulders. "Decided not. That's what you and Dad brought back from your vacation?"

"One of the things, yes."

Carolyn came up to Mirror Head and touched it. "I don't like it," she said. "It's creepy. It looks like a dead person, something that's going to come alive at night and eat us."

Amy laughed. "That's what you get for watching all those zombie shows."

Carolyn moved off down the hall toward her room. "I'm serious, Mom. It's totally creepy."

The younger daughter, Ally, twelve, found Mirror Head fascinating in a scary way. "I'll bet it's evil," she said.

Ed was unimpressed with Mirror Head's display, but said little about it. He had learned long ago that when it came to Amy's decorating ideas, the best course of action was silence. Nothing ever lasted long, as she was always changing her mind. Hopefully, the head would find its way into a closet soon. Or the garbage. To him, Mirror Head looked like it belonged at a funeral—or some dark ritual in a horror film.

Three days later, Ed found Amy in the kitchen fussing over pots of brown and dying plants.

"I don't understand what happened," she fumed. "They were fine until this morning. I got up, and look! It's like they've been left outside without water weeks." She lifted up dry, crinkled, lifeless leaves. "And we've had this one for *years*."

Ed made a sympathetic sound. "Maybe you forgot to water them, or the pots leaked."

"When have I ever forgotten to take care of the plants?"

"Just suggesting possibilities." Ed moved toward the back door, on his way out to work.

Amy quickly disposed of the plants. She, too, had to leave for work. The kids were already on their school buses.

She hurried to the living room with a rag to wipe off the console table where Mirror Head rested. As she wiped, a cold breeze swirled around her. Somewhere in the house, a door slammed. Odd, she thought. No windows were open.

Amy replaced the dead plants with new ones, fresh and shiny, bursting out of their brass colored pots.

The new plants lasted three days, and then Amy awakened in the morning to find them dead and dying.

"I don't get it," she said to Ed. "How could this happen, not once, but twice?"

"Maybe the head doesn't like plants," Ed said drily. "I vote for the closet."

"I am not putting it in a closet, especially considering what we paid for it," Amy retorted.

"Whatever. I'm just an innocent bystander. I didn't want it in the first place." Ed headed for the back door. It was Saturday, and he was off work. "I'm going over to Ben's," he said. "He has a new fly reel."

Amy disposed of the latest dead plants. She went back into the living room to study what she could use for replacements. No more plants.

As she entered the living room, a darting gray movement caught the corner of her eye. It was a vague shape about three feet tall. With it a feeling of nausea swept over her, and passed. Amy assumed it was a trick of light, and something she had eaten at breakfast had upset her stomach.

She tried out various objects on either side of the head, looking for the right fit. It was such an odd and commanding piece, and so large, that it was difficult to find pieces that would complement it.

In the end, she gave up. Maybe she would leave the head alone on the table. She stood looking at it, pondering her options.

Suddenly, as though an ice pick had been stabbed in her brain, an alien thought manifested.

I don't like plants, and I don't like you.

The thought was so forceful that it made her stagger back. She put a hand to the side of her head. *Where did* that *come from?* she wondered.

Just as quickly, she had a rational explanation. *It's Ed and the girls*, she thought. *They've planted silly notions in my head, and it's my imagination running away.*

After that, however, Amy avoided spending time in the living room. Whenever she had to pass through it, she hurried along. Always, a fog-like shape darted out of view.

The other members of the family avoided the room as well. Not that they gathered there much. The girls had their cell phones and video games that kept them busy in their rooms a great deal, and the television was in the adjoining family room. Even so, they all were in the habit of using the room from time to time.

Not anymore. The room was always cold now, colder than the rest of the house, no matter how high the heat was turned up. It had a forbidding atmosphere, as though a hostile presence had taken over.

One night Amy and Ed had friends over for dinner. Amy planned to serve drinks and appetizers in the living home. She anticipated admiration and conversation over her great find, the head.

When the guests arrived and were seated, their gazes fell on the head and froze, looks of uncertainty and astonishment on their faces. It was the opposite reaction from what Amy expected.

She gestured at Mirror Head. "Well, yes," she stammered. "We, ah, found that in a little shop on our trip. Very unusual, don't you think?"

The friends nodded without a word. They didn't need to speak—what they were thinking was written on their faces. One of the women rubbed her arms as though cold.

Ed stepped in to rescue the awkwardness. "I have a great idea, honey, why don't we move into the family room where I can build a fire in the fireplace?"

As they gathered things up, Amy saw the gray blob. It flashed in her vision in front of the head, and then disappeared.

Mirror Head had been in the house for about two weeks when the nightmares and bedroom visitations started. First they involved the younger daughter, Ally.

One night Amy was awakened by a tapping on her arm.

"Mom, Mom, wake up," Ally repeated in hushed tones. She as standing by the bed.

Amy sat up with a start. Ed came awake, too.

"What is it?" Amy said in alarm, thinking an intruder was in the house.

"I'm having bad dreams," Ally whined. "Horrible dreams, and there's something in my room."

"Something in your room!"

"I don't know what it is!" Ally started to cry.

"Let's go," said Ed. He was already out of bed, charging down the hall.

Ally's room was empty. Nothing appeared disturbed.

In halting words, Ally described having a nightmare in which ugly beings were ripping up humans with long knives. When she woke up, a gray blob was standing beside the bed.

"It didn't have any head or eyes, Mom, but I knew it was looking at me!" Ally said. "When I got up, it slid into the closet."

They all inspected the closet, but nothing was amiss.

The commotion awakened Carolyn, who came into Ally's room. When she learned what was going on, she shrieked, "I was having a bad dream like that, too!" She asked Ally to describe the gray blob. "I've seen it, I've seen it! It's been all over the house. Mom, Dad, what is it—a ghost? A demon?"

Ed and Amy calmed the girls down. Ed explained why the nightmares could be normal dreams, and glimpses of blobby shapes were only the imagination, fueled by dreams and by other sources such as television shows and movies.

Amy remained silent about the gray blob she was seeing. She did not want to further alarm the girls.

Then a new supernatural doorway opened. Like a virus that spread, Amy and Ed began suffering nightmares. Amy was plunged into a dark cycle of horrible, violent dreams, drenched in bloodshed and filled with severed body parts. They woke her up in fright in the middle of every night. There was a night light in the master bath that shone dimly into the bedroom. Whenever Amy opened her eyes, a small gray blob in the room zipped away and vanished through a wall.

Ed announced that he had been having bad dreams, and he too, saw a rapidly moving gray blob.

Ally no longer wanted to sleep alone in her room. She begged to sleep in the master bedroom with her parents, even on the floor. They rearranged Carolyn's room to make space for Ally. The nightmares continued.

Misfortune set in. First small things started going wrong: minor mishaps, trials at work and school. Objects inexplicably fell off their shelves at home and broke. No one ever saw them fall—the objects would be found in pieces on the floor. Carolyn went into hysterics one day when she found a favorite figurine broken on the carpeted floor of her bedroom. She immediately accused Ally of playing with it, something she had forbidden, but Ally denied it and the two screamed at each other until Amy broke up the fight. Amy examined the pieces, and could not understand how such a small and light object could break apart like that even by tumbling off the shelf onto the thick carpet.

Small appliances stopped working. Car tires went flat. Every member of the household became ill with respiratory problems that would not clear up. Amy felt fatigued all the time. Ed complained of headaches. They both felt grumpy all the time and snapped at each other.

They heard scratching sounds on the walls at night. Thinking they had mice, Ed called an exterminator. The man found no signs of rodent infestation, or any invasion of small animals who might scrabble around behind the walls.

Even more alarming, sometimes there were multiple gray blobs, not just one. They always vanished almost as soon as they were seen. They were all about the same size, about three feet tall, and semi-transparent. Whenever they were seen, they left a trail of ugly energy behind them.

One day as Amy rushed through the living room, her glance fell on the reflection of Mirror Head in the opposite wall mirror. The glittering face looked impassive, but she had the feeling that somehow it was sneering at her.

A realization exploded on her. *Of course! It's the head!*

Stunned, Amy sat down. She was not a believer in the paranormal, nor was Ed. Now she was seriously entertaining the notion that the head—an object—was the source of all the bad and strange things that were happening to the family. Everything started after the head was brought into the house.

"I told you that thing was bad luck," Ed said when a nervous Amy had explained her new theory to him.

"Do you think something came along with it? Like a bad spirit?"

"I don't know," said Ed, "but that thing is going in the trash."

"No!"

"What?"

Amy shook her head vehemently. She had the strange notion that throwing Mirror Head out or destroying it would be the wrong thing to do. What if the head went—and whatever lived in it stayed behind?

John Zaffis studied Mirror Head and ran his hand along the headband of crystals. Touching the head gave him a feeling that he was connecting with a malevolent and intelligent energy. "That's exactly what you've got, a head with a spirit attached to it," he told Amy. "Everything you have described fits a pattern that we see in haunted objects."

"I'm glad I found you," said Amy, her voice full of relief. She had arranged for John to come to the house when the other family members were out. "What kind of spirit? A ghost? Is it a demon?"

"It's definitely not friendly," John said. "There are low-level demonic-type spirits that like to mess around with people. They can do all the things that have happened to you and the rest of the family. There are more powerful spirits that do the same things."

"Really? Even the nightmares, and all the bad luck?"

John nodded. "That's just the start of it. If you had let it go on, things would have gotten worse."

Amy, nervous, wringed her hands. "I don't understand why a spirit is there in the first place. We buy lots of second-hand things—this house is full of stuff we've bought at antique places and flea markets. We've never had anything like this happen."

"Just because something is second-hand or old doesn't mean it has a spirit attached to it," said John. "Sometimes attachments occur because of the energy of a previous owner. A spirit gets attracted to a person and is able to hang on to one of their possessions. It goes wherever the object goes. Sometimes spirits are called in by people who experiment in spirit summoning, or they use a Ouija board or something like that. They don't close the door when they are done, and the spirit stays."

John looked down at Mirror Head, still sitting in its original spot on the table. "Judging from the way this was made, it was intended to call in spirits. It has even been hollowed out for them. Something got called in that stayed."

"But how could a bad spirit get in? It has a crucifix in the back."

"Some bad entities have a way of getting past barriers," John said. "I've had many cases where religious objects have been used to summon in negative entities." He continued, "When you brought this head across your threshold, the entity was able to get loose and start causing problems. They feed off humans. Your emotional energy, and your fear."

Amy recoiled in shock.

"The energy of being scared is like a food to them," John said. "Whenever they can upset people, or make them sick, they get energized."

John pointed to the two mirrors on the walls. "You've got some things going on here that are making the situation worse. Mirrors can be doorways for spirits to enter the world. You've got bits and pieces of mirror doorways all over the face of this. You've probably heard that breaking a mirror brings seven years of bad luck. So, you've got a substitute for a person—the head—covered with many doorways, and cursed with bad luck."

"I had no idea," Amy said.

"That's not all," said John. "The two mirrors you have on the wall look into each other. That's also not good. Mirrors that look into each other create a funhouse warped space that magnifies openings for spirits.

That's why you were seeing more than one gray shape. Other spirits were able to get in because of all the energy going on."

"Oh my God, we could have had an army of them in here," said Amy. "I should have let Ed destroy it."

John shook his head. "Not a good idea. When you destroy the house of a spirit that's loose, it attaches to something else, and sometimes to a person. And, it usually gets angry and acts up even more. The situation becomes very serious. Sometimes I have to call in clergy to help."

"I'm taking these mirrors down right now," said Amy. She was already in motion, removing first one mirror and then the other from the wall. "What should I do with them?"

"I'll treat them," John said. "They should be fine, as long as you don't hang them up to look into each other again. Any mirrors, not just these two."

"And what about the head? I don't want it in the house, I don't want it anywhere near this family! Is it safe to get rid of it? Will you take it?"

"I can take it and make sure that it never bothers anyone again," said John. "I have an entire building filled with haunted objects."

John said prayers over the two wall mirrors and treated them with sea salt and holy water. He wrapped up Mirror Head and placed it in a box. Back home, he unwrapped it and placed it outside. He treated the head with ample quantities of sea salt and holy water, and said binding prayers over it to contain the entity. Binding prayers act like energetic bonds or chains, preventing an attached spirit from getting loose and affecting people or an environment. He then left Mirror Head to sit out in sunlight for several days. Sunlight cleanses and purifies negative energy.

When the spirit was contained, John moved Mirror Head inside to his Museum of the Paranormal, a collection of haunted objects. Visitors who pass near the head still feel a creepy vibe seeping from it. Some are afraid to touch it, as though the energy will cling to them. Others bold enough to handle the head also feel the heavy energy.

John's collection of haunted objects of all kinds has built up during more than thirty years of paranormal and demonic case investigations that have taken John all over the country and abroad. Thousands of haunted objects are squeezed into the museum. They keep arriving, some by mail anonymously, sent by people who do not want to talk but just want to get rid of the source of their bedevilment. Household items, art objects, clothing, jewelry, ritual and religious objects, games, furniture, masks, dolls, you name it—anything can pick up a spirit hitchhiker who acts out when ushered into a new home.

Mirrors figure frequently in haunted object cases. In our first book, *Haunted by the Things You Love* (2014), we featured a mirror that served as a spirit doorway, enabling shadow beings to enter and plague a household, and mirrors that were involved in two cases of demonic possession. There are many mirrors in John's museum. As noted, badly placed mirrors can create doorways for entities. Such unfavorable placements include mirrors that reflect into each other, mirrors at the head or foot of a bed, and mirrors that are at the side of a bed. Ideally, a person should not be able to see themselves in a mirror while in bed. In occult lore, a person is more vulnerable to spirit activity during sleep. This is borne out in the documentation of entity visitations and attacks, which occur most often when a person is asleep. Sometimes, mirrors that have spirit attachments have no unfavorable placements, like the mirror in *Haunted by the Things You Love*, which hung in a dining room.

Mirrors are not automatically a haunting problem. Everyone has one or more mirrors in their home, and we are surrounded by mirrors everywhere in public. Many people sleep soundly and peacefully with mirrors in their bedrooms. Mirrors used constructively for psychic purposes, such as black mirrors, are not negative. Black mirrors have black shiny surfaces instead of silvered ones, and are good tools for psychic exploration and training.

Extensive folklore about mirrors points to cautions with them in many cases. For example, in earlier days when more people died at home and were laid out at home for wakes and burial preparation, mirrors were turned over. If the dead saw themselves in a mirror, it was believed, they would become confused about being dead, and would remain in the house instead of going out along with their bodies at burial time. Silvered mirrors are considered to be soul-stealers and even soul trappers.

The case of Mirror Head ended well for the family. After John removed the head, Amy and Ed called in a priest and had their house blessed. They had no further activity.

Some "demon haunted" cases, however, do not resolve as easily.

2

Demonic Images

Does a mere image of something demonic or evil have the power to haunt and possess? Some might think so, based on their reaction of fear and revulsion when seeing horrific faces and forms.

Images are used in occult work, and when they are used for particular purposes, such as summoning and contact, they acquire an energy that can indeed spill out and affect others.

The velvet demon face

The scene in the attic was not the sort of thing a person wants to find when they move into their new home. Brad could not ignore it—serious occult activity had taken place in the very sanctuary he had purchased for his pregnant wife and young child. What was he going to do now?

Brad climbed back down out of the attic and slammed the pulldown stairs back into the ceiling. He could ignore it. He could clear it out. He could bring in the priests.

Brad decided first to ignore what he found in the attic, and later get around to clearing everything out.

It was not the right decision.

Brad remembered the day they first saw the house.

From the outside, the small, white salt box house sat innocently on a shady street in a tidy Cape Cod, Massachusetts town. By the time Brad and Kayleigh looked at it, they had been home shopping for weeks and the dozens of houses before this one had blurred together. There were so many nice homes with great features—but none popped as "the" one. As Kayleigh's pregnancy advanced, the couple became more intense about their house hunting. Their goal was to be in place and settled by the time the baby arrived. This was number two; they had a daughter who was two.

It was a sunny but cold winter afternoon, late in the day, and the sunlight had slanted in through the windows at odd angles. The house's owners were out.

The interior was more appealing than they had anticipated, despite the clutter and jumble of furniture. The rooms were spacious with a nice traffic flow, and the walls and dark wood flooring were in good, but not great, condition. They envisioned the placement of their furniture and talked about how the rooms could be used. The house had two stories and an unfinished basement. They looked in all the rooms on both floors, and went down into the basement.

One of the bedrooms upstairs looked as though someone had trashed it. Things were piled and strewn about. The walls had strange symbols painted in black and red on them.

"Teenagers," the real estate agent said in a dismissive voice.

"Yes, I can see this room will need some redoing," Brad said grimly. "Why are these people moving?"

"They outgrew the house," the agent answered. "They have eight kids."

"*Eight kids!*" Brad marveled. "In this little house? Where did they fit them all?"

"Who knows?" the agent said. "It's not my business. It's my job to sell houses and help people find the right new house. This house has a lot of the things you are looking for—price, size, neighborhood." She moved Brad and Kayleigh down the hall. "There's an attic," she said. "It's a large storage space. Do you want to see it?" She indicated a rope that was attached to a trap door in the ceiling. "The stairs might be a bit tricky."

Kayleigh put her hand on her back and declined. She looked at Brad. He shrugged. "I don't think it's necessary right now," he said.

Before they knew it, they had agreed to make an offer and put a binder down on the house. Their offer was quickly accepted by the sellers, who were moving to another town, without a counter offer.

Brad assured Kayleigh that he would take care of all the details of the sale and moving so that she could rest. During the next weeks while the sale progressed, he made several trips to the house to measure wall spaces and to size up what needed to be done before they moved in. He forgot about the attic.

On one occasion, he met the outgoing family. They had a dark, furtive energy about them, as though they were keeping secrets and did not want to have prolonged contact with him. Not all of the children were present, but there were two teen-aged sons who eyed Brad with sullen looks and did not respond to his weak hello.

Their father jammed a thumb in their direction. "They don't want to leave," he said as if to excuse their rudeness. "You know how kids are."

Brad nodded and tried to muster a smile. They must be the ones with the trashed-out bedroom. That one would be the first to be repainted. Get rid of that ugly crap on the walls.

The family did not wait for closing to move out. In fact, it seemed they were in a hurry to leave, now that they had buyers. That was okay with Brad—it was easier, and more pleasant, for him to go to the empty house to continue his calculations for the move.

Brad had to take care of these tasks after work, and sometimes that made for long evenings. One night, he was alone in the empty house, measuring and calculating for some possible renovations. There was no electricity, and so he was working by flashlight. He had a powerful lantern that he set on the floor. It lit up a portion of the living room with a cool light, and cast jagged shadows around the walls where the beam hit angles. The heat was set on minimum to keep the pipes from freezing, and it was cold enough that Brad had to keep his jacket on.

Brad was deeply engrossed in his work when he became aware that there was a regular thumping sound going on. When it first registered on him, he thought it was outside, but as it went on, he realized that it seemed to be coming from somewhere inside the house. He tuned in and listened. The sound emanated from upstairs.

Was there someone else in the house? The doors had been locked and there was no sign of forced entry—but if someone had figured out the house was empty, had they somehow managed to get inside? He edged closer to the front door in case he had to make a speedy exit.

"Hello?" he called out in a loud voice. "Is anyone there?"

Thump... thump... thump...

The thumping was interspersed with a rustling sound.

Must be an animal, Brad thought. "Hello?"

The sounds continued. *Awfully loud for a critter*, Brad thought. He grabbed his lantern and a hammer he had brought along to pound some loose nails in cupboards, and started upstairs. Steps creaked beneath his feet.

Brad shined the lantern up the stairs. He reached the second floor and put the light up and down the hall of the bedrooms. Where were those sounds coming from?

The thumping sounded again, loudly. Now Brad could ascertain that it emanated from the ceiling. The attic!

He moved to stand beneath the trap door in the hall ceiling and put the lantern beam on it. The rope cast a shadow on the wall.

Boom! The noise was louder now. It was followed by rustling sounds.

Brad held his breath, debating whether to pull down the attic stairs. *Gotta be a raccoon or something that got in*, he thought. It would not be a good idea to confront a wild animal in the attic. He heaved a huge sigh of relief and headed back downstairs. He would let the real estate agent know so that she could alert the owners, and have the problem taken care of.

The thumping and rustling sounds continued. Brad was now a bit spooked despite his conclusion, and he hurried to finish up. When he shut the front door behind him, he could have sworn some invisible force pushed him out.

The real estate agent informed Brad there was no animal infestation in the attic. He shrugged off the news. He was glad there was not an animal problem, but he was too busy to contemplate any other explanation for the weird noises.

He made several more nighttime visits to the house, and each time, the thumping and rustling sounds started up. They were unnerving, but Brad did his best to ignore them, as well as his growing unease. Maybe it was a plumbing or vent issue. He would look into it.

The house inspection showed no problems with the plumbing, furnace, or air conditioning. The inspector went up into the attic and saw what was there, but made no mention of it. He thought the items were personal belongings that were supposed to be there.

At the last minute, an issue came up with the title to the house and delayed progress, but was sorted out. Not long after that, Brad and Kayleigh were the owners of the house. They were thrilled.

True to his promise, Brad handled all the logistics of the move-in so that Kayleigh could stay focused on her pregnancy and getting items for the nursery. Still the attic remained unexplored, way down on the list of Brad's to-do priorities.

The move-in did not go smoothly. Brad and Kayleigh did not hire professional movers in order to save money, and instead rented a straight truck and recruited some friends. Several trips would be required to move everything in, but it was still cheaper than professional rates.

Move-in day seemed jinxed from the start. Minutes after driving the truck off the rental lot, the electrical system failed and the engine went dead. Brad lost time while the issue was sorted out. He had to go back to the lot and get another truck. There were none immediately available, and he had to wait for a return to come in.

Brad was already exasperated by the time he arrived at the house with the first load. He was further frustrated to learn that some of those who had promised to help were either late or had, at the last minute, dropped out. He stewed that he might have to keep the truck a second day, running up the costs.

Brad began ordering the helpers who were on hand, barking at them like an army sergeant. His friends were not pleased. As the boxes and furniture went out of the truck, Brad yelled if he thought something was not being handled properly. Arguments broke out.

"If you don't like the way we're doing this," said one friend, "then hire somebody!"

Furniture was damaged and some household goods were broken. When Brad started yelling again, two of his friends stomped off.

Kayleigh tried to smooth things over, but Brad remained in a sour mood.

Finally, everything was in the house, and the task of putting things into place began.

The problems were not over. Three days after moving in, the water heater broke and poured water into the basement. Boxes and furniture that had been taken to the lower level were damaged.

"How could this happen?" Brad asked the repairman. "This heater is not that old. It's practically new!"

The repairman shrugged. "These things happen. I have no explanation."

There were more issues. The furnace quit working and the household temperature plunged. Brad could not find a repair service to come immediately, and had to send Kayleigh and their young daughter to a relative's home.

Every time the couple thought their issues were resolved, something else happened. As they tried to settle in, problems erupted with electrical connections. Outlets went dead, and sometimes the lights flickered throughout the house.

Brad began to think the house was cursed in some way.

One weekend, after the living quarters were set up, Brad decided to tackle the unexplored attic and see how he could he could make use of it. As he pulled down the stairs, a foul odor rushed out. Brad put his hand to his face. *Christ, what's up there?* he thought.

Of all the possibilities that ran through his mind, none of them were what he found.

At one end of the attic was what appeared to be an altar with items on it. Hanging over it was a large painting of a twisted, demonic face surrounded by a black background. Crumpled papers and bits of things were scattered about on the floor.

Brad moved closer to inspect everything. The altar was a rickety, wooden thing, poorly handmade out of cheap wood and unsteady to the touch. On its top were a small chalice, and small candlesticks with partially burned and misshapen black and red candles. The wax had obviously melted and reformed, probably due to seasonal heat in the attic. There also was a disk made out of resin that had a crude upside-down pentacle painted on it. Spatters of black and red candle wax spotted the flooring.

Next to the altar was a pile of dusty books. They were old and musty-smelling. Brad could see by the titles that they were books about demons and summoning spirits.

The small things scattered about the floor near the altar were bones. Brad picked up several and examined them. They were dry and brittle, and appeared to be animal bones. He threw them down in disgust.

He opened up two of the crumpled balls of paper. They were covered with the same strange symbols he had seen painted on the walls of the teens' bedroom, along with inscriptions for summoning spirits with odd names.

The most disturbing item of all was the huge ugly face over the altar. It had been painted on black velvet. It was clearly a demon, not human, painted in a garish neon yellow. The eyes were red, and its red-lipped mouth was open to reveal long vampire-like fangs.

Suddenly the air in the attic was swirling with dust. Brad convulsed in violent coughing, a choking sensation in his throat. He felt nauseated.

He had to get out. He scuttled back down the stairs and slammed the trap door shut.

"It was those kids," Brad said, as he and Kayleigh discussed his hideous find in the attic. He was referring to the teen-aged sons whose bedroom had been the trashy one. "I *knew* there was something wrong with them!" *Satan freaks*, he thought to himself. He did not say the word out loud because he did not want to alarm Kayleigh.

Kayleigh had a worried look on her face. "Is—is there something in this house? Is that why we've had so many problems?" She rested her hands on her belly in a protective measure.

"I'm getting rid of that stuff right away," Brad said.

Brad armed himself with a dust mask and a large empty box and returned to the attic. Working quickly, he scooped up the papers, books, bones, and altar items and chucked them into the box. He took the box downstairs and put it in the trunk of his car. Then he returned to the attic with another empty box, and dismantled the rickety wooden altar. Those pieces went into his trunk as well.

For some reason, Brad could not bring himself to touch the velvet demon face. He could not even look at it. He left it in the attic.

He drove to the dump and sent the contents of both boxes into the refuse pile. There! That took care of the matter.

It did not, as Brad was soon to discover.

The supernatural activity in the house increased dramatically. There were more problems with the appliances and electricity. The washing machine mysteriously overflowed. Faucets turned on full blast by themselves.

Even more distressing, the house was filled with disturbing sounds at night: creaking noises, as though someone was walking up and down the stairs, and a return of the weird thumping sound Brad had heard when he had been in the house by himself. On several occasions, Kayleigh woke up in the middle of the night to the sounds of whispering voices. When she returned to sleep, she had terrible nightmares.

Now she was clearly frightened.

Brad sent Kayleigh and their toddler back to the relative's home for temporary shelter while he dealt with what was now a full-blown supernatural outbreak. He had no idea what to do, but he figured a religious remedy was in order.

He contacted a minister recommended to him. The church was fundamentalist evangelical. The minister agreed to bring a group over to pray the evil away in a deliverance. He told Brad there was something in his house that had an evil spirit attached to it.

The small group of men and women were quiet and somber as they filed into the house. Under the minister's direction, they went first to the basement and moved methodically through every room in the house, praying aloud and calling out for the evil to be expelled in the name of Jesus. The intensity built.

In the attic, the group recoiled at the sight of the demon face.

"This is where the Devil lives!" the minister exclaimed, pointing to the painting.

While the prayer group thundered away, Brad thought the house itself was in agony, as though it were trying to vomit up a poison.

The aftermath was like the eerie calm that descends in the wake of a hurricane or tornado. Brad was drained. The prayer group departed, their job finished. The minister blessed the house and warned Brad that things might get worse before they get better. "Get that painting out of the house," he said.

Brad nodded. He still could not bring himself to touch the painting.

Brad decided not to bring his family back right away. He wanted to make sure that the house was free of malevolence. Something still did not feel right.

He slept that night on the sofa in the living room with the television on. He had disturbing dreams, and was jarred awake by a loud crashing sound. His first instinct was that someone had broken into the house. He jumped up, heart pumping, and reached for a baseball bat that he had put beside him.

A cautious search of the house showed nothing amiss.

Boom! A loud noise sounded upstairs.

That's it! Brad thought. *No more!*

He stayed awake the rest of the night, listening to the random noises that sounded throughout the house. When the gray light of dawn showed through the window blinds, he rose, steeled himself and went up into the attic.

The velvet demon face loomed out of the semi-darkness, leering at him. It seemed the expression on the face had changed—or was it just his paranoia? Brad yanked down the painting and hurried out of the attic and house as fast as he could. He set it outside against the garage.

Brad discovered John Zaffis and called him, spilling out the entire story.

"You did the right thing to get it out of the house," John said, adding that he would get there are soon as he could.

"Do you think those boys painted this themselves?" Brad asked while John examined the painting.

John shook his head. The painting was crude but not amateurish. "Looks like those velvet paintings you find at flea markets," he said. "You know, Elvis and those types."

"But who would paint such an ugly thing?" Brad said. "And sell it?"

John shrugged. "Go figure, buddy. But I'll take care of it." He treated it with sea salt and holy water sprinkled on the frame, and said prayers over it. He wondered why anyone would buy a house without first inspecting every part of it, and why anyone would leave something like this in an attic once it was found—but sometimes people make odd choices. He remembered a case involving a woman who purchased a home with an obvious magical working room that had a floor painted black and red with the image of a Baphomet (see the story below) on it. The woman used it as a bargaining tool to get several thousand dollars knocked off the price of the house—and then paid the price of a horrible haunting that was difficult to resolve. Some people treat the occult like cartoons.

Back at his own home, John left the painting outside for several days, his customary practice of letting sunlight do some purification. The painting felt inert, and so he did not perform a binding. Whatever had infested the house, if it had been attached to the demon face, was gone.

John hung the velvet demon face up in the barn that houses his Museum of the Paranormal collection. It has never given him any trouble, though visitors find it creepy and full of "bad vibes." Perhaps it's just the appearance of the twisted, ugly face that gives people the chills.

About a year later, John was able to have a follow-up call with Brad, and was glad to hear that the house was free of activity. Brad told him that he had confronted the former owner, the husband, and asked point-blank about demon-summoning, the altar, and demon face painting. The man was uneasy and vague. Well, yes, he admitted, a couple of the kids had gotten fascinated by the occult and kept stuff in the attic. He insisted that nothing bad had ever happened in the house, and "the boys got over" their fascination. He passed it all off as minor, and suggested that Brad's pregnant wife might have been highly strung and "over emotional."

Privately, John suspected that the boys had gotten deep into the occult, far more than their parents either knew or wanted to admit, and had been able to summon up something that landed in the house and would not go away. Perhaps that was why the family moved. However, the problem was resolved—at least for the present—and only time would tell if anything would be able to creep back in.

John heard nothing further from Brad.

Moral of this story: when shopping for a new place to live, inspect every part of it. If you find what appear to be occult symbols or drawings on the floors or walls, ask hard questions. Bring in experts if necessary. Proceed with caution.

The Baphomet

Baphomet is one of the most widely recognized of all occult symbols, and one of the most frequently used in devil-themed horror films. It is the symbol of the satanic goat. Baphomet is portrayed as a half-human, half-goat figure, or a goat head.

The origin of the term "Baphomet" is unclear. It may be a corruption of "Mahomet" or "Muhammad." The English occult historian Montague Summers suggested it was a combination of two Greek words, *baphe* and *metis*, or "absorption of knowledge." Baphomet has also been called the Goat of Mendes, the Black Goat, and the Judas Goat.

In the Middle Ages, Baphomet was said to be an idol, represented by a human skull, a stuffed human head, or a metal or wooden human head with curly black hair. The idol was allegedly worshiped by the Order of the Knights Templar as their source of fertility and wealth.

The best-known representation of Baphomet is a drawing by the nineteenth-century French occultist, Eliphas Levi, called "the Baphomet of Mendes." Levi combined elements of The Devil card in the Tarot and the he-goat worshiped in antiquity in Mendes, Egypt, which was said to fornicate with its women followers as the—just as the Christian Church claimed the Devil did with witches. The image appears in Levi's book *Dogme et Rituel de la Haunte Magie (Dogma and Ritual of High Magic)*, published in 1854.

Baphomet acquired its greatest notoriety from The Church of Satan, founded in 1966 in San Francisco, which adopted a rendition of it to symbolize Satanism. The symbol is a goat's head drawn within an inverted pentacle, enclosed in a double circle. In the outer circle, Hebraic figures at each point in the pentagram spell out Leviathan, a huge water serpent demon associated with the Devil.

Baphomet, by Eliphas Levi (1854)

Does the image of Baphomet hold some terrible power? The image itself will not exert a negative effect. It will not make people go crazy or cause them to be possessed. But if someone has used a particular image of Baphomet for occult purposes, such as summoning, that image can absorb those energies. The residues may be strong enough to impact an innocent person who acquires it—like Shania.

In her early teens, Shania was fascinated by the occult and wanted to flirt with the dangers of it—or at least the danger she perceived from her exposure to the exaggerated portrayals of it in film and fiction. One day while she was browsing in a consignment shop, Shania spied a nickel-sized pendant of a Baphomet, made out of cheap metal and strung on a chain. It was mixed with similar jewelry in a dusty old display case. She was immediately intrigued with it and simply had to have it. She had no idea what it was, but it looked cool, was certainly unique, and seemed to be occult in nature. Something for her friends to envy.

Shania took it home and then started wearing it every day. She knew her mom, Tess, a devout Catholic, would not approve, and so she made sure that the necklace was well hidden by her clothing when she went out of and into the house.

After a few weeks, Shania started experiencing strange activity on her person and in her house. Whenever she wore the Baphomet, she felt electrical pulses shoot through her body, which all seemed to originate from the necklace itself. The energy penetrated into her chest and then distributed to all her limbs, as though she were a big electrical network.

Shania also began to experience horrific nightmares on a nightly basis. Terrifying black-hooded figures menaced her. She became frightened of going to sleep, and tried to stay awake all night. She was not successful, and soon took on a haggard and listless appearance. Shania realized something bad was happening to her beyond her control, and decided it was time to confess to her mom.

Tess was not pleased. She did not know the name of the image—Baphomet—but she knew that it looked evil to her. "This is a symbol of the Devil!" she shrieked at Shania. "What have you done?"

Tess had heard of John Zaffis, and she wasted no time looking him up and contacting him. She described the pendant her daughter had been wearing and the strange sensations and nightmares she was having.

"That's Baphomet," John said. "It's a symbol used in a lot of satanic worship. Even though Shania is innocent, it could still cause big problems for her if it was used in a lot of rituals."

"Oh my God," Tess moaned. "Can you please come over as soon as possible? Help my little girl!"

John cleared his schedule so that he could visit the household right away. When he arrived, Tess had laid out the pendant on the kitchen table. She called in Shania to speak with John.

With eyes cast down toward the floor, Shania explained, in a voice barely above a whisper, how she had found the pendant and started secretly wearing it. When John pressed her for details about the nightmares, she would only respond, "They're nightmares you never want to talk about."

John sensed an energy of an attachment in the pendant. Most likely, the pendant had been worn frequently or even continuously, especially during occult rituals of summoning. Something demonic had lodged in it, and was dormant until Shania started wearing it. Her own energy, her life force and vitality, was enabling this spirit to awaken and feed off her. If she were to continue to wear it, the energy would increase to the point where worse effects would manifest.

"It's good that Shania stopped wearing this," John said. "You should remove this from the house. Spirits attached to objects can jump into a house energy."

Tess looked horrified. "I don't want it anywhere near here," she said. "Take it away, destroy it, whatever! I never want to see it again!"

John inspected the house and did not feel a house exorcism was needed. He removed the object and treated it with sea salt, holy water, and binding prayers, and placed it in his museum.

Shania and Tess and their home had no further trouble. Shania decided to avoid the occult, and, with her mother, renewed her faith.

3

Demon Haunted Things and Places

Any object or place can become attached by a variety of spirits and entities. Some offenders are quite malevolent and others are more on the pesky side. By "demon haunted," we mean any attachment haunting, or possession of an object or place that is disturbing to the living, with effects ranging from mischievous to detrimental to life-threatening.

Earth is full of the demon haunted. Human reality intersects with the astral plane, where many entities reside and where the afterlife is located, and also intersects with parallel dimensions attached to the earth. Parallel dimensions, a concept in the "many worlds" theory of quantum physics, holds that other-dimensional realms are right next to ours, existing at different vibrational frequencies.

From a paranormal perspective, this theory makes a great deal of sense. We encounter occupants of other realms and experience weird phenomena when doorways or windows open between our world and theirs. These openings may be spontaneous and temporary, and dependent on a host of factors, or may be ongoing, such as in "hot" areas called portals.

Spirits and entities

The demonic realm

Most of the spirits that attach to objects come from the demonic realm. In popular thought, "demons" are evil forces working under the direction of Satan. The demonic realm is much more complex, however, and populated by a wide variety of entities that range from trickster to evil, with plenty in between. In addition to the demonic entities themselves, there are other beings and spirits that have been called "demonic" because they have been believed to be in league with the Devil.

The broadest and most inclusive definition of a demon is a type of spirit that interferes in the affairs of people. The term "demon" comes from the Greek term *daimon*. The ancient *daimones* were both good and evil, and even included deified heroes. They exerted positive and negative influences upon people.

In the Western magical tradition, demons have comprised a broad range of intermediary beings of varying dispositions and temperaments. They can be summoned for help and to carry out spells and even useful tasks. In magical books, or grimoires, they have sometimes been called "spirits." They are blamed for all the misfortunes, diseases, and ills suffered on the planet by man and beast. The most malevolent ones are capable of possession, the effects of which range from mental disturbances and influences to a full, physical overtaking of a person or animal.

In Christianity, demons have their origins in the fallen angels who followed Lucifer, or "morning star," when he was cast out of heaven by God (Isaiah 14:12) for being prideful. In the New Testament, Jesus healed by casting out demons, in keeping with prevailing traditions. By the end of the New Testament period, demons were synonymous with fallen angels, all under the direction of Satan, the figurehead of ultimate evil that evolved as Christianity developed.

As Christianity spread and overtook other religions, the pagan gods, goddesses, faeries, and nature spirits were incorporated into the ranks of demons or at least allied with them. Witches, spellcasters, and magical adepts were also said to be in league with demonic forces.

Demons create many problems. They can cause haunting phenomena, invade dreams, cause illness, and create unpleasant smells and sounds. They are shape-shifters and can appear in many guises, including alluring ones, but usually they are associated with hideous and terrifying forms, especially black ones. They are capable of giving off great stenches. Possession cases are plagued by powerful demons of this type. They are quite dangerous and can be difficult to exorcize.

In the Christian worldview, demons are soldiers of Satan and are dedicated to subverting souls. They are the embodiment of all things evil and hateful. When confronted in exorcisms, they spew anti-Christian and foul language.

Elsewhere around the world, however, demons—even malevolent ones—might behave differently. They might exhibit foul behavior, but their rhetoric is different, and some of them will cease and desist when exorcists cut deals with them. (In Christianity, striking a bargain with a demon is selling one's soul to the Devil.) Some demons might be more like sly tricksters, or self-serving when it comes to picking on humanity.

The bottom line on all demons is that they are a source of trouble. Many of the ones that attach to objects are low-level entities and not the powerhouses found in possession cases. They can still cause plenty of problems, however, and are not to be underestimated, for they can increase their strength when they are loosed in an environment, or have the opportunity to attach to a person.

Djinn

Elsewhere in the world, especially the Middle East, the demonic entities are known as Djinn, which means "the hidden ones." Djinn are ancient supernatural beings who ruled the planet before humans were created, and they were pushed out, according to the Qur'an, because they would not bow to Adam. They retreated to another realm, which in modern terms is a parallel dimension.

The Djinn are not universally malevolent or evil, but are more like humans, a mix of good, bad, and ugly. The ones most likely to interact with people are hostile, however, and act in ways similar to demons. They have many agendas ranging from pestering people to destroying them. Like demons, they can be summoned and employed.

Both demons and Djinn are everywhere on the planet, and are not limited by country, race, or culture. They mold themselves to the places they inhabit, and in accordance with the beliefs and customs of humans. Westerners are not familiar with the Djinn, but they are active in the Western world. Both of us have dealt with numerous Djinn cases.

King Solomon summoning Djinn to do his bidding

One of their favorite forms is shadow people, completely black silhouette humanoid forms that usually look like tall men (six to eight feet in height). Sometimes there is a suggestion of a coat, hat, or cowl/hood. These figures are bedroom invaders, terrifying people by appearing at the foot or side of the bed in the middle of the night, exuding great malevolence. Sometimes they attack people by jumping on them with choking or suffocating effect.

Shadow people also show up in intensely haunted areas such as portals, described below. They are capable of attaching to individuals and also families through multiple generations, and they are associated with extraterrestrial abduction cases.

Faeries and elementals

Faeries, like Djinn, once had dominion on the planet and lost out to humans, according to lore. Faeries share many of the same characteristics as Djinn: they are shape-shifters, have varying dispositions, and possess supernatural powers. Many have a low regard for humans. They are capable of creating havoc when they have been wronged by people.

Elementals are spirits associated with the elements of Earth, and rarely interact with humans.

Faeries and elementals are more likely to be anchored in places than attached to people, though some faeries develop fascinations with people and will follow them around. Their antics are more mischievous than harmful, but when they are angry at people for violating their land and space, they can wreak great havoc and ruination.

Elementals are encountered in attachments to places, usually when a house or structure has been built on land they occupy, or they somehow become displaced.

Spirits of the dead

When humans pass from the earthly plane to the afterlife, they leave behind residual or shell energy. This energy can cling to places and personal items, especially if there was a significant emotional attachment while the person was living. This energy fades over time.

In some cases, the energy is strong enough to have an effect on people. The individuals may pick up on the previous owner's personality, moods, and even physical conditions, and mimic them. Our story "The Enchanted Walking Stick" is an example of this.

In some cases, the dead seem to be actively attached to a place or object. There are two possible explanations. One is that they are earthbound and have not made their full transition. Souls can become earthbound due to disorientation or shock at the time of passing, fear of the afterlife, or an intense emotional desire to complete business on earth. The second reason is that the object may serve as an energetic link to the living, and enable someone on the Other Side to act out in the physical world, such as in cases where they disapprove of how a favored object or place is being treated.

Thoughtforms and projections

Energy from the living—including emotions and thoughts—can contribute to the creation of thoughtforms, a type of artificial entity that, if sufficiently powered, can take on its own personality. Thoughtforms must be constantly recharged to stay viable, and if they are not, they fade and die away like a drained battery.

It is not likely that thoughtforms alone can create a negative haunting, but they may be part of the mix. Thoughtforms might also be energized by spirits and entities that are drawn to certain active or haunted locations.

Living people are capable of projecting powerful psychokinetic energy that can literally create haunting phenomena, including objects that move, fly, and disappear and reappear. These are usually temporary episodes. See our chapter on "The Mystery of Walkabout Objects" for more on this complicated phenomenon.

Portals

The house was magnificent. The property—spectacular. The price—amazingly affordable. But ever since moving in, Janet felt like she was in a combat zone. Except the militants were not humans.

Instead, Janet, her husband, Sean, and their two teenagers found themselves in daily and nightly warfare with unseen terrorists of the paranormal kind, invisible entities who upset the order of their household, wrecked their sleep, frightened visitors—and made them feel distinctly unwelcome.

Creepy shadows moved around the rooms both day and night. The couple felt constantly watched by unfriendly eyes. Objects went missing or were moved to strange locations without explanation. Appliances and lights malfunctioned. Presences came into their bedroom at night to stand at the foot of the bed—or even climb up onto the bed. Whispery voices sounded in parts of the house.

The family took a stance of trying to ignore the activity, figuring if they paid no attention "it" would go away.

"It" did not.

As the months wore on and the couple got to know their neighbors and the area better, they made a disturbing discovery: they were not alone in their discomfort. In fact, the homes in a wide area around them were plagued with similar problems. And, there seemed to be an extraordinary level of human chaos as well. Janet and Sean were always hearing about marital discord, fights, separations and divorces; financial problems; and substance abuse. Granted, those issues pop up wherever human beings congregate, but they felt like they were in a fishbowl of excessive and constant turmoil. What was more, there always seemed to be bizarre accidents happening in the homes and out on the roads.

One day, Janet was running errands and ran into a neighbor. The woman politely asked how the family was doing in their new home. For reasons she could not explain, Janet felt prompted to comment on the unusual undercurrents in the house. "I think we have ghosts," she said with an uncomfortable laugh.

To her surprise, the neighbor did not laugh it off. "That's what the previous owners said," she replied. "Nobody seems to stay in that place very long."

Shaken, Janet went home filled with a new dread. She decided to do some research, and made an unsettling discovery. The house indeed had a history of frequent turnover of occupancy—and so did some of the other homes in the area. There were old newspaper clippings of murders, suicides, and accidents in the area. According to old folklore, the woods were haunted and mysterious lights bobbed about in them. More recently, mysterious lights in the sky—UFOs—had been reported. Janet wondered if her family had inadvertently stepped into a real-life twilight zone.

She was partially right.

And now the big question was, could they do anything about it?

In our decades of paranormal investigations, our case files are filled with accounts like these: people who move into homes with the expectation of domestic comfort and happiness, only to find that their new place is already inhabited by presences who are not pleased to share the space—and have no intention of leaving.

Super-charged active areas are called portals, or doorways, because they have high levels of ongoing paranormal activity. Such places are "demon haunted," not necessarily by evil beings defined by Christianity, but by troublesome and hostile beings or presences that have the power to make life miserable for the living.

Patterns

Portal activity follows predictable patterns. Some people put up with as much as they can stand, and then move. Others hunker down and learn to live with it. Some try to get rid of the phenomena, treating the presences like paranormal pests. They call in ghost hunting groups, exorcists, priests, shamans, psychics, demonologists—a parade of paranormal experts who all have differing opinions on what is going on, and who advise different remedies. Many remedies work only to temporarily dampen things down, and not to permanently resolve the problems. The main reason why is that portal openings never close. Activity may wax and wane, but it never completely ends.

In earlier times, people intuitively sensed these areas and either avoided them or learned how to coexist with the entities who populated them. Today, most people do not think about the consequences of occupying an interdimensional crossroads—or, if they do, they assume they have eminent domain and the right to push out anything they do not like physical, spirit, or otherwise. The otherworldly residents do not always agree.

Personal encounters with the unexplained range from startling to terrifying, and they are all part of a much bigger picture. Portal places where the veils between worlds are thin are everywhere. There are so many on earth that one could argue that the entire planet serves as a gateway to Somewhere Else. Indeed, we may be at the crossroads of some cosmic highway. The very place you are living in may be part of a portal to another dimension, a doorway to another realm where entities share the planet with humans but are seldom encountered, except when conditions are right. Those conditions involve place—the energy of the land—and consciousness—what is going on in the minds and energy fields of people.

Planet earth, planet portal

Planet earth is a complex habitat. We live on a little planet, but to us it is immense, with a staggering variation of topography and climate. Some areas are more hospitable than others, but humans have learned over the millennia to take hold and survive almost anywhere. We consider the Earth our domain. Wherever we plant our foot, we have a right to stay.

Earth, however, is much more than physical geography. It is honeycombed with invisible doorways to other dimensions that are layered around the physical space we live in. These dimensions have their own residents, who we interpret as spirits, demons, nature beings, mysterious creatures, ghosts and poltergeists, faeries, angels, aliens—the list of labels is long.

For the most part, we all stay in our own domains most of the time. We may have the odd experience here and there when a "window" between worlds flies open and we have a paranormal experience. In portal areas, the interdimensional space is more fluid. The residents of other realms can access ours—and we can do the same, glimpsing their realms.

There are many different kinds of portal areas. Some offer spiritual experiences, while others generate discomfort. The portals penetrate both physical and psychic space. They connect different dimensions. They last, in human terms, for very long periods of time, and some have spanned centuries of human history. Portals are not imaginary spaces and places. They are literally anchored into the land.

Ancient peoples all over the planet understood portals. In earlier times, people were more psychically sensitive to their landscapes, and molded their societies around the energies of place. They may not have understood portals in our modern quantum physics terms of parallel dimensions, but they did understand that "other worlds" existed alongside ours and intersected with ours at various points.

The ancients understood that these intersections needed to be respected and accommodated. Human culture had to be suited to place, which was spirit-filled, and not vice versa. Failing to do so meant the different between a healthy, long, and prosperous life, and a life filled with trauma and disaster.

So, people avoided problematic places, which often spawned legends of cursed lands, or lands belonging to invisible beings. In faery lore, for example, we find many cases of "no trespassing" signs hung out by the faeries, and woe be unto the humans who violated that understanding. The faeries would make sure that misery of bad luck, bad health, and even death came to such reckless or ignorant people. If you were foolish enough to build your house on top of an invisible faery house, it would fall down into ruin—and so would your life.

Ancient peoples turned pleasant portals into sacred sites, and built temples and places of pilgrimage where they could invite interaction with the gods. Shrines, healing temples, dream incubation temples, holy wells and springs, sacred mountains and lakes, divination caves, and places of worship have been constructed in portals.

Today we have terms for this natural sensing of the landscape. Among them are geomancy, which means divining the energy of the land, and feng shui, the art of placement according to natural energies.

The ancient Greeks and Romans understood that there were "good" places and "bad" places that were the "haunts of spirits," and the wise person respected that, especially by avoiding the bad places lest their health and lives be ruined. The Romans had a specific name for the spirit that inhabits a place: *genius*. In particular, the genius is a guardian spirit that animates a locale and gives it unique powers and atmosphere. The genii do not travel back and forth between realms, but rather exist in the spaces between realms. They can be encountered in certain active areas when a person is in the right state of consciousness. As guardians, they are territorial. We find in modern cases that people who visit or inhabit portals often come up against beings who are quite territorial, and are willing to make a point about it. There are far more than genii out there.

Geophysical signatures

Portals have one or more certain geophysical characteristics. One is marked magnetic anomalies. Many of the portal areas have high concentrations of magnetic content to the soil, such as iron, magnetite, and quartz. Other characteristics are underground water, especially if it comes to the surface; natural caves; mining tunnels; large bodies of water, especially running; and swampy areas.

In addition, portals are often on lines of earth energy called leys, which are alignments and patterns of powerful, invisible earth energy connecting various sacred sites, such as churches, temples, stone circles, megaliths, holy wells, burial sites, and other locations of spiritual or magical importance. Leys have not been proven scientifically, but they can be dowsed. From an occult point of view, the energy of leys can bend dimensional space so that portals open at certain points on the earth.

Besides geophysical factors, portals are influenced by activity in the earth's magnetosphere, the phases of the moon, the seasons, the times of day and night, environmental factors—and the biggest wild card of all, *the consciousness of people.*

Human events

The residues left by human activity can contribute to portals. Sites of battles, accidents, murders, and suicides imbue a place with negative and unhappy residual energy that can turn into haunting activity, or can draw low-level entities that feed on such energy. Burial sites that are forgotten and then disturbed can contribute negative energy. Sometimes, as noted, traumatic activity is influenced by the physical energy of a portal area—it becomes difficult, if not impossible, to separate the chicken from the egg in determining which came first. Does a traumatic event happen because of the negative influences of the land, or does an event contribute to the land energies? It may be a case of both.

The Salem, Massachusetts witch panic of 1692, may be an example of this. Salem was founded by a band of Plymouth, Massachusetts settlers who came to America to escape what they felt was the tyranny of the Church of England. The settlers who split off from Plymouth felt that colony was too lax. In 1926, the separatists sailed along Cape Cod to the mouth of the Naumkeag River, liked it, and established another colony. "Naumkeag" was a local Indian term meaning "eel land." The name of the new colony was later changed to Salem.

From the natives' point of view, the settlers made a bad choice. The land was considered cursed and unfit for habitation. From the beginning, Salem was an unhappy place, full of hardship, jealousy, and rivalry. Added to that was a religious oppression that was still fueled by Inquisition fears of witchcraft. Salem combusted in 1692 in a hysteria of witchcraft accusations that led to more than two hundred incarcerations and twenty executions. Much of the haunting activity that remains in Salem and its environs today still stems from the witch trials.

The neighborhood next door

Thousands upon thousands of portals, many of them "demon haunted," or problematic, may connect our world to other worlds. Some portals are famous, such as the Hudson River Valley that we discuss in this book, while others are smaller and known as local haunts or mystery spots, or simply places where weird things happen.

The spread of humanity has led to a steady encroachment of the land. More and more, the interdimensional portals are overrun with people who come to stay. And some of the invisible residents protest in response.

In the following pages, we present more stories of haunted objects, afflicted people, and haunted land.

4

Relics of Painful Deaths

The dust of mangled, collapsed buildings and incinerated human beings was still floating in the air when souvenir hunters descended upon the wreckage of the World Trade Center towers in Manhattan in September 2001. Some of the hunters were shell-shocked and wanted a piece of what now was a memory, the twin towers of the WTC, one of the great symbols of American wealth and prosperity, destroyed by hijacked jumbo jets that were flown straight into them. Some had friends and family members who perished in the disaster, and they wanted something tangible to connect them to their lost loved ones. Other souvenir hunters had more mercenary interests, calculating that bits of the rubble would fetch them a nice profit.

The souvenir hunters did not stop to think whether their finds might come with a price of their own, something that would destroy the peace of their homes and invade the sanity of their minds.

When photographs were published of the towers as they burned, billowed smoke, and fell down, people gasped. There in the clouds and pillars of smoke and ash reaching out into the sky were images of demonic faces, mocking the tragedy. Skeptics dismissed them as simulacra, the perception of something recognizable in a meaningless background—but others more familiar with the ways of the spirit world and paranormal phenomena knew better. Spirits find opportunities in the material world to make their presence known, including impressing a likeness onto a natural background. The lords of darkness had spoken.

Security forces moved swiftly to cordon off the disaster scene, but pieces of debris were strewn all over lower Manhattan. Many of those pieces were taken home by untold numbers of people.

Lower Manhattan, the heart of the financial district, has had a long reputation for being haunted. Some of the oldest streets and buildings are there, and residual phantoms and phenomena dating to the early settlement days of the city roam the streets and occupy the buildings.

In the immediate wake of the World Trade Center disaster, new phantoms and phenomena were experienced throughout the district, especially close to Ground Zero, by rescue and recovery workers, law enforcement, emergency medical crews, and the people who lived and worked in the area. Ghostly forms of people in business attire, looking confused and sad, were glimpsed, and phantom sounds of the disaster itself, as well as the screams of terrified and dying people, were heard.

Debris from the WTC site was carted off to various landfills. On Staten Island, a landfill site with the ironic name of Fresh Kills received ten tons of debris, where crews of sifters combed through it for body parts and for personal items that might help to identify the dead. There, many workers saw the ghostly form of an African-American woman dressed like a World War II Red Cross volunteer, carrying a tray of sandwiches. At first glance, some took the woman to be a real person, helping the sifters in their grisly task.

One of the witnesses who saw the ghost was Sergeant Frank Marra, a now retired NYPD Assistant Chief Officer who was among the first responders, and helped in the recovery efforts. Marra described his experiences in his book, *From Landfill to Hallowed Ground: The Largest Crime Scene in America* (2015), co-authored with Maria Bellia Abbate. When Marra realized the figure was a ghost, it hit him "like a ton of bricks," he said.

A psychic told him the figure was a spirit guide that was helping victims cross over to the afterlife. In the aftermath of violent, sudden death, some souls are lost, confused, or too shocked to make an immediate transition. They need help.

The ghostly Red Cross figure was not the only phantom seen. There were other apparitions, as well as dark figures, shadow forms, and dark masses that radiated an ugly energy. The denizens of the demonic realm will always come to feed on the grief, anger, and terror expended in a killing, especially a mass killing.

The sifters at Fresh Kills recovered 54,000 personal objects. Tens of thousands more items were reclaimed by sifters working at other sites. Some of these objects, including bits of wreckage, were given to families, friends, and colleagues of the victims. For some, the objects became cherished mementoes to be displayed or put away in a safe and secret place. For others, the objects invaded their homes with something quite unpleasant.

The cross

Gary was among the recipients of a wreckage memento. He had lost his partner in the disaster; his body was never recovered. He was presented with a small piece of one of the towers, two pieces of welded steel that formed a small cross. The metal was twisted and had the appearance of being partially melted. For its small size—about four by five inches, it was incredibly heavy. *It must weigh at least a pound,* he thought to himself.

Gary could not bear to have a reminder of the disaster around him, visible every day, forcing him to contemplate how his partner might have died. He preferred not to think about that. Still, he wanted to keep the cross, so he stored it away in his basement.

Whenever he went near the box that contained the cross, Gary felt strange, as though he were caught in some powerful force field. It was a distressing sensation. On more than a few occasions, he hurried to finish his purpose in the basement and then literally ran upstairs.

The basement did not confine the energetic presence of the cross. The force field crept upstairs, spreading like a dark stain. Unexplained phenomena started—subtle things at first, then more dramatic. Gary heard whispers coming from rooms, as though a group of people were gathered in his apartment. There were strange scraping sounds and thuds. Sometimes he awakened in the middle of the night feeling as though someone were standing in the bedroom—but no one was visible. He soon felt watched almost all the time he was in his apartment. The air seemed heavy and oppressive.

Finally, Gary could stand the discomfort no longer. He knew he did not want to keep the cross. He wanted to put 9-11 behind him, but the cross reminded him of it every day, even as it sat in a box in the basement. He knew it was there.

Gary sought out John and offered him the cross. "I want it to go to someone who will know how to take care of it and give it the proper respect," he told John. "That person is you."

When John took the cross in his hands, a weird feeling swept over him. For a few moments, he was taken back in time to September 11, 2001, and he was reliving the horror of that day. It was as though the cross contained and embodied the disaster, like a paranormal hologram.

An odd memory floated to the surface, of a man whom John had met in connection with a paranormal case. Suddenly the man had gone quiet, and did not return phone calls or answer emails. Then John learned that the man had been killed in the WTC disaster. John was struck by the fragility of life, and the suddenness with which it can end. For some reason, he knew he did not want anyone else to touch this cross relic that Gary had given him.

John had the cross mounted in a shadow box. For a long time, he kept it put away, not on display. Then he got it out and placed it among his collection in the museum.

Today the cross conveys horror and sadness to those who come near it. Even if people do not know where it is from, they sense grief and heaviness about it.

Gary's cross is not the only piece of WTC wreckage to absorb energy from the tragedy. In 2011, the National September 11 Museum was opened at the site of the disaster to commemorate the 2,977 people who perished that day. The exhibitions featured wreckage, photos, videos, recovered personal items and clothing, and more. One twisted piece of steel girder, taken from the location where American Airlines Flight 11 smashed into the North Tower, was noticed to feature a face. The face appeared to have wide open eyes and a mouth open as if in horror. It was dubbed "The Angel of 9/11." The face gave people the chills, and some did not want to go near it.

More than a decade later, debate still goes on about the role of the dark forces in the World Trade Center disaster. Were the perpetrators demon possessed, or, more likely, Djinn possessed, using religious and political excuses for a demonic assault upon the human world? Are all such acts of violence, including war and aggression, instigated and egged on by the dark side?

There are those who believe so.

All deaths are tragic in their own way. Death does not need to happen on a mass scale in order for objects to acquire an unhappiness or even malevolence, either through the residues of the newly dead and the trauma of their passing, or the attachment of an opportunistic spirit.

The battered license plate

In 2004, Tom, a volunteer firefighter in a small town, responded to an emergency call about a working fire. He jumped in his car and sped off down the road.

His wife and children never saw him again.

Tom never made it to the fire. His car was struck by another vehicle and he careened out of control, smashing into a tree. Tom was killed on impact.

After the funeral, Tom's widow, Mary Alice, was presented with a memento from his fellow firefighters. They had retrieved the license plate from his car, and gave it to her.

It was an odd gift, but Mary Alice accepted it gratefully. She placed on an end table in her living room, propping it up for display.

But something was not right.

Maybe it was just her grieving process, but Mary Alice never felt right about the license plate. It gave her the creeps. Every time she looked at it, the battered plate reminded her of Tom's horrible accident, and made her contemplate his final moments. She did not want to disrespect the gesture of his fellow firefighters, however, so she left the license plate in its place on the table. Maybe, she thought, she would get over those feelings as time went by.

She did not.

Mary Alice tried moving the license plate to different rooms in the house, places where she was not likely to see it as often as in the living room. It didn't help. She still tensed upon seeing the plate, and was flooded with unhappy memories.

Strange things started happening in the home. Lights went on and off by themselves in whatever room contained the license plate. At first, Mary Alice would enter the room, knowing that she had left the lights on or off, and then find them reversed. Lights that were on were off, and vice versa. She was tempted to blame the kids, but incidents with the lights happened when she was alone in the house.

Then Mary Alice noticed that objects seem to relocate on their own. She tried to convince herself it was her forgetfulness, and she had done it herself—but that didn't work, either.

What was going on? Her house was going insane on her.

Mary Alice did not believe in the paranormal. The only possible explanations for these odd events had to be "normal" ones. There were none.

One evening, Mary Alice entered a room and turned on the lights, and her eyes landed on the license plate. Right in front of her, the license plate flipped off its stand and landed on its face. She stood frozen, aghast. It was as though unseen hands had seized it.

That was the final straw. Mary Alice found John Zaffis and called him.

When John arrived, she handed him the license plate. "If I hadn't seen it with my own eyes, I would have never believed it in a million years," she told him. "I can't have this in the house anymore. It keeps reminding me of Tom's accident, and besides…" She hesitated, then went on, "I have the weirdest sensation that Tom is somehow attached to it. I—I want Tom to be at peace."

John explained that the dead often reach out from the Other Side to let family and friends know they are all right. Common phenomena are lights and appliances going on and off, displacement and movement of objects, and personal signs. "If someone's passing has been sudden or tragic, they might also be earthbound, or stuck, for a while," he said.

The idea that Tom might be stuck in a strange limbo upset Mary Alice. John gently explained that this is often a temporary condition, until a soul finds its way to the afterlife, sometimes with help. If Tom was trying to send her a message through the activity in the house, Mary Alice could help him by acknowledging that and sending him prayers. The family was Catholic, and so John also suggested that their parish priest be called in for a home blessing, and that Mary Alice request a mass to be said in Tom's honor.

She agreed.

With the removal of the license plate, the home blessing, and the mass, Tom's soul seemed to be put to rest. No further activity disturbed the home. Mary Alice was better able to move through her grief and get on with her life.

The license plate now resides in John's collection, the symbol of a journey that began on Earth and ended in the afterlife.

In the next story, sometimes the living are the ones who create, or at least facilitate, a haunting related to unhappy death. Grief is a powerful force, and it overtakes lives and minds.

The bedroom shrine

It was supposed to be a fun day at an amusement park, but it ended in tragedy.

Earlier in the day, Connie and her husband, Ted, decided to visit the park. They packed a light lunch and bundled up their six-year-old son, Jimmy, and drove off under a sunny sky.

The park was crowded and noisy, and music blared from all the rides and games. But the day turned from happy to tragic when an accident on a ride fatally injured Jimmy. For Connie and Ted, their world would not be the same again.

The day little Jimmy was laid to rest, Connie knew she would never change his bedroom. Somewhere in the back of her mind, she felt that if she did not change his room, he had not died. Something of Jimmy would always be with her.

Everything in the room was left exactly as it was the day he died. His bed remained partially made—Connie had decided to leave it until they returned from the park. All of his clothes remained in their drawers, and his shoes were left jumbled in the closet. His little red jacket for warmer weather remained on a hanger. There was a calendar on the wall; it became frozen in time.

Ted said nothing, figuring this was how Connie needed to work through her grief, and at some point she would be ready to go through the room, save the things she wanted, and get rid of the rest. As the days wore into weeks and the weeks into months, Ted began to doubt that his wife was going to move on. If he mentioned anything about changing Jimmy's room, she went into hysterics, shrieking that nothing was to be moved or changed. She refused to allow anyone in the room except for Ted and the maid. The maid was under strict instructions to dust carefully, and to not move any object from its place.

In the first weeks following Jimmy's death, Connie spent long periods of time in his bedroom with the door closed. Once Ted opened it and found her sitting in the dark. She reacted angrily and told him to leave her in peace.

"Don't ever bother me when in I'm in here with Jimmy!" she shouted at him.

Ted obeyed. Sometimes when Connie went missing from the house, he knew where she was, and if he walked by Jimmy's room he heard her sobbing inside.

Ted's attempts to reason with Connie or discuss her growing obsession with Jimmy's room were rebuffed. Eventually, he stopped trying, and a chasm developed between them.

Years went by. Jimmy's room became a shrine. It was eerie, a room where time had stopped. It was somber and sad.

The room gave the maids who came and went the chills. They saved Jimmy's room for last, and did the minimal amount of dusting as fast as they could. A few refused to go in; Connie fired them.

Over time, the entire house took on an atmosphere of cold and sadness. Connie spent less and less time in Jimmy's room, but continued to refuse to alter it in any way. Visitors to the house were always uncomfortable without knowing why. Some thought the house was haunted. It was—by a heavy, depressed thoughtform that combined Connie's grief with the chain to her dead child. Part of him was earthbound in a strange way, for she had never in her own mind and heart allowed him to move on.

Connie and Ted never had any more children. Over the years, Ted had tried to persuade Connie to move, convinced that a change of locale would heal everything. He also tried to persuade her to enter therapy. She refused both.

They were in their early thirties when Jimmy died. Ted passed away at age seventy-eight.

Connie's health declined as she advanced in age, and after Ted's death, she hired a caregiver. Nancy dreaded going into Jimmy's room. It had an awful feel. The curtains, once so bright and cute, were literally decaying on their rods. The bedding also was faded and dirty. The toys looked forlorn. Nancy often thought she saw a ghostly shadow in the room that lingered around the closet.

Eventually Connie's deteriorating health necessitated her moving to an assisted care facility. Her last words to Nancy as she was wheeled out of the house was, "Keep Jimmy's room."

With Connie away, her relatives decided to clear out the house and sell it. Connie would not be coming back.

No one wanted to clear out Jimmy's room. "It's cursed," one of the workers said, and quit.

Connie's primary caregiver, Nancy, was acquainted with John Zaffis. She knew how clothing could retain energy and memories, and she was convinced that something of little Jimmy remained imbued in his clothes. Perhaps additional imprints of haunting energy had been created by Connie's intense sorrow and guilt.

Nancy removed Jimmy's little red jacket from its hanger. For decades, it had been left undisturbed in the closet. The cloth had a strange feel, and Nancy felt that "something" bad might rub off on her if she held it too long. She stuffed it into a bag and took it to John.

The clothing had more than bad memories clinging to it—it had attracted a low-level spirit that fed off the energy, and contributed more bad energy to the house.

John gave the jacket a cleansing and dispatched the spirit. He added the jacket to his museum, where it joined numerous other garments that had become haunted. Some visitors who have been near the little jacket have had the immediate impressions of tragedy, sadness, and being stuck.

Some psychic imprints never really wash away—they just get duller and duller over time, until at last they vanish below the level of human perception. For this and other reasons, it is a practice with many people the world over to get rid of the clothing of the deceased, along with other personal items.

Not all belongings of the dead have negative effects. Many people keep mementoes for years and have happy feelings when they look at and handle them. There are plenty of problematic objects, however, which is why it is important to heed the warning signs, such as: an unrelenting "heavy" or "dark" atmosphere; the appearance of dark forms or shadows; unexplained sounds and movements of objects; mystery voices; and unpleasant dreams. These and similar symptoms, occurring in combinations, are a sign that an object might be the source of paranormal activity that should be remedied.

5

The Demon Box

Salvatore made an excellent living as a picker, one of the best in his state. He bid on expired storage lockers, and had an uncanny knack for picking ones that contained treasure troves of valuable items. One never knows what lies behind the metal door, junk or jackpot, and every now and then Sal got a rude surprise. Like the day he won the demon box.

The box came from a small locker in a rundown neighborhood, so from the outset Sal had low to modest expectations. It got his attention because it had a cheap price tag, and, curiously, no other pickers either wanted it or paid any attention to it. In fact, the manager of the storage facility had called him with an offer.

"Sal, I've got a waiting list of new customers who want that unit, so it needs to be cleared," the manager said. He explained that it had been rented by an old man who had stopped paying the rent. He vanished without forwarding address or known relatives who might claim the contents. In fact, no one seemed interested in the contents, not even any other pickers, who often inquired about what might be coming up on the auction block. The manager did not know if the old man was alive or dead, but enough time had passed that he was legally able to sell off the contents. He wanted a fast deal and offered Sal an incredibly low price.

Sal took it.

Due to the small size of the locker, Sal figured he could handle clearing it himself, so he set off alone in his truck. He hoped the old fart had stowed an antique or two that would fetch a good price with the dealers, or maybe even an unrecognized gem of a painting. Those kinds of finds did happen, like lucky oil strikes. Old people stashed away amazing things.

When Sal lifted up the metal roller door, a cloud of foul dust exploded out into the air, enveloping Sal and making him cough and choke. *What the--?* he thought. *Smells like a mummy's tomb.* Sal, of course, had no idea what a mummy's tomb should smell like, but surely it would be rank and foul like this.

As the cloud of dust dispersed and settled, Sal was able to peer inside and see the contents. There were stacks and stacks of cardboard boxes of different sizes, all heavily coated with gray dust. *How in the hell did all this dust get in here?* he wondered. *The door has been shut for God knows how long.*

He brushed the top of the closest box, sending another foul cloud of particulates into the air. Whatever the dust was made of, it stank.

Coughing, his eyes tearing, Sal backed off and went to his truck. He got out gloves and a dust mask, and an industrial vacuum.

It took him several hours just to get the dust out. It kept clogging up the vacuum and causing it to shut down. After much exasperation, perspiration, and swearing, Sal cleaned the stall enough to handle the boxes without collapsing from the dust.

By then it was late in the day, and the sun was low in the sky. Sal had the peculiar thought that he should hurry up and finish before the sun set, or... *what?*

Usually Sal liked to inspect some of the boxes and items before he loaded up his truck, but now he was in a hurry to get everything out of the locker and into his truck. He could open the boxes and examine the contents at home.

On the way home, Sal was inexplicably nervous. He kept looking into the side mirrors, as though he expected to be followed. The road usually was filled with a lot of traffic at this time of day, but he drove alone, no one behind him, in eerie isolation. One or two cars going in the opposite direction passed him. *Where was everybody?*

It was dusk by the time Sal reached his place, out in the exurbs. He had land around him, and a good sized outbuilding where he stored his finds until he could resell them. Nobody bothered him. He lived alone. There had been a woman once, but that was a long time ago.

The gathering darkness had a queer feel to it. He felt compelled to get indoors as quickly as possible, as though home was a safe haven against something unknown. *Screw the boxes, I'll do them in the morning,* he thought.

Then he hesitated.

There was one box that had piqued his curiosity. It was plain brown cardboard like all the rest, but when he had picked it up, he felt an energy to it, almost like an electrical pulse. It was very lightweight.

Okay, he would bring that one into the house and go through it.

Sal pawed through the boxes in the truck until he found the one, and took it inside to his kitchen.

He cut through the packing tape on top and pulled out wads of crumpled up and yellowed newspaper. The newsprint had a wretched stale smell. He undid one wad and smoothed it out. *Holy crap! The date on the top of the page was June 6, 1966!*

He pulled out more wads of stinky newspaper, going down deeper into the box, wondering if the box held nothing but newspaper. Finally, way down, he hit something solid and pulled it up. Stripping away the newspaper, he saw the item was a small black wooden box.

He turned it over in his large, meaty hands. It was about eight inches long and four inches high. It appeared to be hand-carved and painted, and then coated with cheap shellac, a lot of which had blistered and worn off. The box had brass fittings at the corners, which were dark with tarnish. One of the brass corners was partially pried off. There was a brass closure on the front.

This was no ordinary old box, however. Heavy amounts of candle wax had been poured in a line where the hinged lid and body of the box came together. All of the joints had coatings of wax. Wax had also been poured over much of the top of the box. A small silver metal cross had been affixed to the center of the top, and was completely covered in wax. The wax appeared to have once been white, but it was now yellowed and stained with age. Sal had the impression that the box had been sealed to prevent it from being opened. But what could be so valuable or important inside to warrant this unusual treatment? He shook it, and nothing rattled.

There was no writing anywhere on the box, even the bottom. Sal fished through the rest of the packing box, but found nothing. There was no explanation for the box's purpose, why it was sealed with wax, and who did it.

As he held the box, a queer and unsettling feeling stole over Sal like damp fog. Suddenly it seemed the overhead light in the kitchen cast sharp and threatening shadows around the room. Night pressed in through the windows. Sal usually liked his solitude, but now he felt very alone in the world. For a moment he was suspended in a trance-like state, and then vigorously regained a clear head.

Sal shook the box again, wondering what was inside that required such a binding. It was as though someone did not want anyone to access the contents. Nothing rattled or slid around. The box might be empty. He was tempted to pry open the wax-encrusted lid—but something held him back.

Sal stood up. It was not late, and he was accustomed to retiring well after midnight, but suddenly he felt exhausted. It must be the after effects of all that crappy dust. He headed for his bedroom, his feet growing heavier with every step. He fell on top of the bed in his dusty work clothes, and descended into a torpor that was filled with nightmares of hideous beings and monsters, and blood-drenched landscapes.

Shit.

That was the first thought that crossed Sal's mind in the morning, and it reflected how he felt. Every joint in his body ached, and he had a dull headache. There was a horrible taste in his mouth, as though he had eaten dirt. When he opened his eyes, everything in the room was triple. He blinked several times and was able to focus.

Sal could not account for his wretched state. He wondered if the dust in the storage bin had something toxic in it. He had certainly inhaled enough of it. He heaved himself out of bed and stumbled to the kitchen to put on a pot of coffee.

The mysterious box sat askew on the little kitchen table, where Sal had left it. He sat down and waited for the coffee to brew, rubbing his eyes and face.

Then he noticed that the kitchen was not in its normal cluttered state.

The pile of dirty dishes and pots that had been stacked on one counter was gone. Looking around, he saw that the objects were scattered around the kitchen in a careless way, as though someone had thrown them. Some of them were even on the floor in the corners. Several glasses were broken. Silverware looked tossed about.

How in the hell did that happen? he wondered. His first thought was an intruder had broken in during the night. How anyone had managed to throw the dishes and pans around without making a racket and awakening him was mystifying. A quick check of the house showed nothing else amiss, and nothing missing, either.

Sal picked everything up, threw the broken pieces away, and tumbled the rest into the sink.

The coffee helped, but he was not hungry. In fact, his stomach felt queasy. Maybe it was the deli sandwich he had eaten the day before for lunch. Whatever.

After several mugs of bitter coffee, Sal decided to finish emptying out the boxes from the storage locker. He unloaded them into his barn and set to work.

It was a disappointing pick, a ringer. Several boxes held old, tattered, and musty clothing suitable only for an incinerator. There were humdrum household objects, most in bad shape. Some of the boxes held peculiar items: a small black cast iron cauldron, large black iron candlesticks covered in wax drippings, a sword and several small knives with strange markings etched on the blades, tarnished and pitted silver goblets, pieces of white chalk, and chunks of incense that had lost most of their scent. There was a large plaster statue of a fierce looking angel wielding a shield and sword, and stepping on the head of what looked like a demon. The colors on the statue were badly faded, and the plaster was dented with numerous chips.

In other boxes, Sal found sheaves of deteriorating paper, bearing scribblings and more strange symbols. They reminded him of astrological symbols, but they were different. There were drawings of circles with pentagrams inside, and undecipherable words and symbols written around them.

Then there were boxes of musty books, all on magic, demons, and rituals for summoning spirits.

So *the old boy was into magic*, Sal thought, now excited with his purchase. His mental cash register kicked into action. *Let's see... a collection of old ritual objects and books from an "unknown powerful wizard" could fetch a good price. People paid stupid money at online auctions for stuff like this. And don't forget that box!*

Maybe Sal had struck a gold vein after all.

A crash of something hitting the floor came from the kitchen. Sal found the mystery box on the floor on its side. Miraculously, it was not cracked, chipped, or broken by the fall. But how had it managed to get from the middle of the table to the floor?

He picked it up and brushed it off, pondering whether he should leave the wax as it was, or try to reseal the box with fresh wax. Fresh wax, though would ruin it as an old object. The box felt strange in his hand, as though it were alive. He quickly set it back down. He would decide later.

Back in the barn, Sal sorted the wheat from the chaff and hauled the worthless items to the local dump. Then he set about cleaning and polishing the magic items, and airing out the books. Even musty, a collector would probably go for them.

The process did not go well.

The cast iron items proved to have abrasive patches that were invisible in the black. Several times Sal flinched and saw he had acquired minor cuts and abrasions. While he worked in the barn, enormous bees kept buzzing him. He swatted at them, and was stung.

The silver goblets refused to polish, no matter how much tarnish remover he put on them, and how hard he wiped. He even dipped them in a solution, but that did little improvement, either.

Sal usually had the stamina of an ox, but now he could not work for long without becoming greatly fatigued. He fell asleep on the spot several times, and had weird dreams and nightmares. He was always disoriented when he awoke.

He thought perhaps he had been overworking in general. Too many projects, hauling too much stuff around himself, doing everything. Or maybe he had a strange virus. Oh well.

He hit the sack again early that night, feeling sick. He was disturbed by bloody dreams and a red-eyed, demonic-looking face.

He came awake in the depths of the night by crashing sounds in the house. He kept a gun in the nightstand drawer beside his bed. He yanked it out and jumped out of bed to investigate.

No one was in the house, and there were no signs of a break-in. Sal put on his boots and went out to the barn, but it was locked and all was quiet outside, save for the noises of night insects and creatures.

On his return to the house, he noticed that the little box was missing from the kitchen table. Immediately he was slammed back against a wall by a tremendous force. The wind was knocked out of him.

Oddly, he thought he heard laughter—but it was inside his head. And it was going to make him *crazy*.

After that night, Sal felt watched in the house, in the barn, and on his property. Everywhere he went, a pair of unseen hostile eyes followed him. Whatever it was, he could almost hear it breathing.

His house was now invaded by shadows that slid along the walls and floor, even the ceiling, and then disappeared. Sometimes they were blobs, sometimes they had vaguely human shapes.

Sometimes they slid into cupboards and closets. But if he had the nerve to open them, nothing was there. The shadows invaded his bedroom. Every night, when he collapsed into an exhausted sleep, the last thing he saw when he closed his eyes was a shadow form slinking into the room.

From a colleague, Sal heard about a local man who collected magical items and books, who might be interested in the entire collection. The man insisted that Sal bring the items to him; he refused to travel to Sal's location. Sal was still feeling sick and even dizzy at times, but he agreed. He wanted to be rid of everything from that storage locker. He decided in advance that he would not say anything about the weird things that had been happening at his place, the nightmares, night-time disturbances, anything that might queer the sale. This guy might be a collector, but you never know what is going to freak out a person.

He unpacked and unwrapped the items and laid them out on the lawn in front of the man's house. The man had declined to allow Sal inside. "My apologies," he said, "but I have my reasons."

Sal was good at reading the body language of prospective buyers, and he could tell the man was not pleased by what he saw. Even though the man kept an impassive face, he still had small cues and gestures that betrayed his thoughts. A lump formed in Sal's gut. This was going to be a tough sell.

The man's eyes roved over all the objects. He did not touch anything. Then his gaze fell on the little box that had been waxed shut. By now, Sal was privately calling it "the demon box." It kept relocating itself throughout his house, without natural explanation.

The man pointed to the box.

"Yes, go ahead and pick it up," Sal said. "You can examine anything."

The man shook his head. "No, you pick it up."

Whatever. Just buy the damn thing, Sal thought. He picked it up. It felt like a piece of lead. That was another bizarre thing about the box—it kept changing its characteristics.

"Now let me see the sides," said the client. "Yes... now the bottom. Right... now hold it closer so I can see the top." After a few moments, he said, "Has anything happened to you since you acquired these items?"

Sal bunched his shoulders. "Why, nothing..." he started to lie, and then within a few moments, all the events came tumbling out of him. He could not stop himself. It was cathartic, a release of internal pressure.

The man looked Sal in the eye. "I want you to take all these things away. I am sorry, I will not be acquiring them. I'm going to give you the name of a man you need to call. He will know what to do."

John Zaffis steered his car up the bumpy dirt road leading to Sal's house. It was midsummer, and yet there was a curious stillness—even lifelessness—to the area. As the house and barn came into view, it seemed to John that a black pall hung overhead. He had seen that pall before, in cases where a nasty entity was on the loose and wreaking havoc.

Sal looked weary and disheveled. His eyes were dull. John quickly picked up on the presence of a malevolent entity in the heavy atmosphere inside.

Sal had all the items collected into open boxes on the floor of his kitchen. The demon box sat on the kitchen table. John poked through the boxes while he listened as Sal told him the entire story.

"The guy I tried to sell this stuff to wouldn't touch anything," said Sal. "You're not afraid?"

John shook his head. "Some people are sensitive, or they are worried they will pick up something from the objects. I do this all the time."

"There's the real problem," said Sal, pointing to the demon box.

"Yes, I know," said John. He picked it up. "The purpose of this box was to imprison an entity—a spirit or a demon. It was captured into the box, and then shut and sealed with the wax, along with incantations and prayers."

"People do that for real?" Sal asked incredulously.

"Since ancient times," said John. "Spirits can be trapped in any kind of container—bottles, jars, boxes."

John went on, "Judging from all the items and the books, the old man who owned these things was a practitioner, someone who conjured spirits. He might have done it alone, or been part of a ritual group. It's dangerous to summon demonics—they can go out of control. The old man probably summoned up an entity that created a lot of problems and would not go away, so he was able to capture it into the box. As long as the seal is not broken, the entity is imprisoned indefinitely."

This was a great deal for Sal to take on board. First, he didn't believe in real demons and spirits. Second, this man Zaffis was telling him that his box that was probably empty was a jailhouse for a demon.

Sal's mouth worked while he struggled for words. He remembered how he had thought about breaking it open.

John read the look of puzzlement on his face. "If an entity that is bound into a container gets loose, it creates a lot of issues—phenomena, nightmares and things like that."

"But I had those things happen!" Sal exclaimed. "I didn't open it!"

John held the box close for him to see, and pointed to the wax seals. The one that ran along the front of the box had a hairline crack. "Did you drop it?" John asked.

Sal's eyes widened. "No... but I found it on the floor the first morning, like it had fallen off the kitchen table somehow."

John nodded. "That's how it got loose." He went on, "The entity is still attached to the box—it's been its home. It's a good thing you didn't let this go on much longer, or it might have been able to attach completely to something else in the house, or to you."

Sal was still looking shell-shocked. "Take the box. Get it out of here. Take everything!"

John treated the demon box with sea salt, holy water, and prayers, and performed a binding, an energetic seal that was far more effective than wax. He could feel a great deal of resistance from the unseen presence, a battle of wills.

John also treated the house and the barn. He recommended to Sal that he call in religious help to do both an exorcism of the property and of his person.

John loaded all the old man's magical items into his car and departed for the long drive home. The demon box rested on top of a pile of papers. En route, the car started bucking, as though the engine were choking in fits. John had to pull off to the side of the road twice and invoke spiritual assistance to end the trouble.

He left the items and the box outside in the sun for several days. The other items had residues of energy that were easily cleansed, but the box retained a powerful force. He performed another cleansing and binding and left it outside again, until he was satisfied that the entity was bound and neutralized.

The box rests in John's museum with a brooding presence, giving those who come near it the chills.

6

Foul Things in Containers

It was a small bottle, but, from an occult perspective, it was as potent as a nuclear bomb. It was a spirit trap, now unearthed from its grave in a woman's front yard.

What was inside it?

John had responded quickly to the urgent phone call from the homeowner, a woman named Anna. When he arrived, the bottle was sitting in the yard, near the hole where Anna had found it while gardening.

Anna's home was small and neat, a classic white New England house with dark blue shutters. From the outside, it looked serene and inviting, the kind of cozy home one might find on a post card or in a travel brochure.

Inside, the house was a different story. It had a dark past, full of frightening activity and ugly, black forms that had assaulted the occupants.

For reasons Anna did not acknowledge, the house had become haunted by a force that everyone felt was demonic. It made horrible scratching sounds on the walls, thumps on the stairs, and it invaded her bedroom and landed with a crushing weight on her. Everyone in the family suffered from violent nightmares.

In desperation, Anna reached out to paranormal experts for help, but no one was able to provide lasting relief. Investigation groups had trooped in and out with arrays of equipment, and every visit seemed to make whatever was lodged in the house angrier. At last she had found "the shaman," as she called him, not giving his name.

"He told us that we had an evil spirit in the house," Anna explained to John. "He said we had been cursed by someone who had a grudge against my husband. Something related to business."

The shaman told Anna he would get rid of the spirit and then cleanse the house.

"When he got out this bottle and his herbs and things, I thought it was crazy," Anna said. "He was going to put a spirit in the bottle? But he seemed to know what he was doing."

The shaman said he needed to work by himself in the house while he performed the capture. The family departed and returned in a few hours. They found the shaman sitting on the front steps of the house, his bag of working tools beside him. He looked serene, as though he could wait there for days.

He told them he had removed the spirit from the house and had done a cleansing, and they would not be bothered anymore. He did not say what he had done with the spirit, or where it went—Anna really did not want to know, anyway.

The shaman was right. From then on, peace reigned inside the house. Anna was relieved.

Months passed, and now, on this sunny day, while she was digging around in the yard, Anna's little spade hit a solid object. When she pried it out, she was astonished to find the very bottle that the shaman had brought with him to trap the demonic spirit in their house.

A sickening feeling swept over her. The shaman had buried the bottle in a shallow hole right in her front yard by the steps! All this time, the "thing" had been right under their noses!

John looked at the bottle. It was small, about five or six inches in height, and resembled a medicine bottle. The glass was clear. Inside, settled on the bottom, were bits of what appeared to be hair, some seeds, and leaves. They were topped with an oily liquid, which was in turn topped by a thin, dirty watery liquid—probably from seepage in the ground. The bottle had no top, but the opening had been covered with a bit of aluminum foil that was sealed with clumps of wax. The foil was dried and brittle, and loose.

John picked the bottle up and tilted it to inspect the contents more closely. The foil top fell off, and the liquid poured out, splashing on his hands and onto the ground.

Jesus!

Whatever had been imprisoned in the bottle was now out and might be capable of lashing out. Immediately, John went into his "protection mode," with prayers ad invocations of spiritual help for himself, the house, and the family. He washed his hands and treated them with holy water and sea salt, and did likewise on the ground where the liquid had fallen.

When the situation seemed under control, John carefully placed the bottle in a container to be removed from the premises. He would place it in his Museum of the Paranormal. He told Anna to call him right away if any activity started up in the house again.

The house remained quiet. John surmised that the foil seal had broken while in the earth, and the spirit—if it had been contained in the first place—had escaped some time ago. Perhaps in his cleansing, the shaman had created a protective barrier that prevented it from re-entering the house.

Questions remained. Why would a skilled practitioner entrap a spirit and then not put a proper cap on the bottle? It should have had a tight lid that was sealed all the way around with wax, not just in several clumps. And the bottle definitely should not have been buried in the victim's yard. When spirit bottles are buried, it is in a distant location, and deep enough so that the bottles will not be disturbed. An imprisoned spirit that is accidentally released might attack or attach itself to someone innocent.

For John, the episode reminded him of the need to always invoke protection at the outset, for one never knows what unpleasant surprises are in store from the spirit realm.

Imprisoned spirits

Magical spells, rituals, and techniques to capture disembodied entities in containers have been in use for thousands of years. There are two primary reasons for doing so: to prevent harmful spirits from wreaking havoc, and to place spirits under one's command for performing tasks. Either way, summoning and capturing spirits is a risky business that often backfires on practitioners. If an attempt to capture fails, or if a spirit breaks free of its bonds, there is literally hell to pay.

To the casual observer, it seems improbable that something immaterial like a spirit can be physically captured and held in a container. If spirits have no physical form, and they can move through walls and solid matter, then how can they be imprisoned?

A force of spiritual energy holds them in place. The force is accomplished through a projection of will and intention that is combined with spiritual elements, such as prayers, the aid of spiritual allies, herbs, incense, crystals and stones, and magical symbols. Many magical formulas have been created over millennia, and are still in practice today. To capture a spirit, techniques call for summoning commands or enticements that lure a spirit. The entity can be seen with the clairvoyant ability of the practitioner.

The objects that serve as the containers can include masks, bottles, jars, boxes, rings, and other jewelry. In fact, almost any container can serve as a "spirit home" or even a "spirit prison."

Devil traps
One ancient example of a spirit prison is the Babylonian devil trap, which was used from about the second to seventh centuries CE. The devil trap was a terra cotta bowl about the size of a modern soup tureen that was inscribed with a magical charm that would ensnare demons or else drive them away. The bowls were turned upside down and buried under the four corners of the foundations of houses and buildings to seal the cracks where demons could sneak in.

Most of the surviving bowl are inscribed in Aramaic or Persian, in spirals that go from the rim to the center. Some of the centers of bowls have a primitive drawing of a demon in chains. Many of the inscriptions call upon angels or King Solomon and the power of the seal of his magical ring (Solomon had legendary control over all spirits, including the Djinn), discussed below.

An example of a charm is the following:

> The demon NTY', TTY QLY'. BTY', Nuriel, Holy Rock. Sealed and countersealed and fortified are Ahat, the daughter of Imma; Rabbi, Malki and Dipshi, the sons of Ahat; and Yanai the daughter of Ahat, and Ahat the daughter of Imma, and Atyona the son of Qarqoi, and Qarquoi the daughter of Shilta, and Shilta the daughter of Immi—they are their houses and their children and their property are sealed with the seal-ring of El Shaddai, blessed be He, and with the seal ring of King Solomon, the son of David, who worked spells on male demons and female liliths. Sealed, countersealed and fortified against the male demon and female lilith and spell and curse and incantation and knocking and evil eye and evil black-arts, against the black-arts of mother and daughter, and against those of daughter-in-law and mother-in-law, and against those of the presumptuous woman, who darkens the eyes and blows away the soul, and against the evil black-arts, that are wrought by men, and against everything bad. In the name of the Lord. Lord, Hosts is His name, Amen, amen, selah. This charm is to thwart the demon Titinos....

King Solomon's magic

In Biblical times, the most famous magician of all for his ability to control spirits was King Solomon, the son of David, who is credited with building the Temple of Jerusalem and much of the city of Jerusalem. Solomon reigned from about 970–931 BCE, nearly one thousand years before the estimated life of Christ. The story is told that when he ascended the throne of the Israelites, God asked him what he wanted. His answer was wisdom. Pleased that he had not asked for power or money, God granted Solomon wisdom and the gift of discernment, and power over the entire spirit world. He is said to have commanded spirits with the help of a magical ring, which he also used in spirit exorcisms.

In Solomon's times, the "spirits" were known as Djinn, a race of supernatural beings that had once ruled the planet and now were consigned to its shadowy side. Solomon enslaved the Djinn and forced them to build his temple. In most ex-canonical texts that feature King Solomon, "Djinn" is translated as "demons."

Solomon was known to imprison the Djinn in containers. Zosimus of Panopolis, a Greek alchemist and gnostic mystic who lived around the turn of the fourth century CE, wrote about Solomon and his powers. Zosimus referred to a lost work called *Seven Heavens*, which described how Solomon used special magical formulas and bottles for conjuring and trapping demons.

The Testament of Truth, a text in the Nag Hammadi Codices, also talks of Solomon's commanding of demons to build his temple. The Nag Hammadi are Gnostic texts written on papyrus that were discovered in 1945 in Upper Egypt near Nag Hammadi, the town after which they are named. They were discovered in ancient jars; some were unfortunately burned as fuel. The Testament of Truth paints an unflattering picture of Solomon as being empowered by the Djinn, or demons, he controlled. He contained them in waterpots, from which they eventually escaped and then plagued the earth:

> They are wicked in their behavior! Some of them fall away to the worship of idols. Others have demons dwelling with them, as did David the king. He is the one who laid the foundation of Jerusalem; and his son Solomon, whom he begat in adultery, is the one who built Jerusalem by means of the demons, because he received power. When he had finished building, he imprisoned the demons in the temple. He placed them into seven waterpots. They remained a long time in the waterpots, abandoned there. When the Romans went up to Jerusalem, they discovered the waterpots, and immediately the demons ran out of the waterpots, as those who escape from prison. And the waterpots remained pure thereafter. And since those days, they dwell with men who are in ignorance, and they have remained upon the earth. (IX,3)

Solomon's vast magical knowledge was said to have been passed on down through the ages, preserved in magical texts that became known as grimoires. Most of these texts were written from the sixteenth century on, even though they claimed ancient lineage; there are historical references from the first century CE to Solomonic texts.

This magical knowledge evolved as a blend of Christian, Jewish, pre-Christian, and occult lore. Grimoires provide instructions for evoking spirits and containing them and commanding them. The containment of spirits also can be found in rural folk magic around the world, and in in Hoodoo and Voodoo, angel magic, Kabbalistic magic, and many other sources.

Genie bottles and rings

The Djinn became known as genies in the eighteenth and nineteenth centuries, thanks to poor French translations of old oral Arabian folktales known as *The Arabian Nights*. Many of the tales, which pre-date Islam, describe how Djinn were magically captured into bottles. If liberated, they were obliged to grant their liberators wishes (three wishes was not necessarily the limit). The French translated "Djinn" as "genie," after the Roman guardian of place, the genius, which we mentioned earlier in this book.

"Genies" have been treated poorly in Western culture. They are objects of amusement and entertainment, not to be taken seriously. They are, however, quite real, quite formidable, and capable of great destruction, including possession. Rosemary has come to the conclusion that Djinn account for many severe negative hauntings, attachments, and possessions. John has encountered the Djinn as well—as we discuss in cases later on in this book.

Today, modern sorcerers around the world capture Djinn and imprison them in vessels and bind them to objects. They usually are put into jars, bottles, boxes, and jewelry. "Djinn jewelry" is sold on the internet with promises that the bound Djinn can be pressed into service for favors. As we have stated, even if one succeeds in getting service out of Djinn, there is a price to be paid for it, and usually an unpleasant one.

Much of the Djinn jewelry offered for internet sale is not genuine, but some buyers do get the shock of a lifetime. The following account was sent to Rosemary from a person who purchased a ring on the internet that was supposed to imprison a Djinn:

The Djinn ring

I had an interesting past few months after purchasing what I thought was a novelty item and not real. I was looking online and found a ring I really liked and for some reason I felt drawn to it or you might say fascinated by its design. I just kept thinking of it for a week and thought that surely by now it had been purchased. I contacted the seller and they informed me it was still available and they would even give me a discount. I asked if the Djinn was real in the ring and they asked if I believed in such things. I took this as a no and due to the fact that the wording on the website said it was purely for entertainment purposes.

I purchased it and it was shipped to me from India... I was astounded that I received it in only three days. I have bought things before from other countries and had to wait a week or more for my items to arrive.

When I opened the box, there it was, and when I put it on I heard sleigh bells begin ringing and it seemed as though they went around and around the room. I thought I was hearing things until I smelled cigarette smoke, and seen a faint materialization of a shadow floating across the wall. I felt paralyzed for a moment and then laughed and said, *Hmm my imagination is getting the better of me today.*

I seen nothing else or heard nothing else for five days and then five days later in the morning I turn my microwave on and it blows up. I mean sizzle, and boom and the door flies open. The smell was terrible like sulfur and hair burning. The same afternoon my TV which is new came on by itself and turned to channel 11 then back to channel 5 and then back to 11 and then switched off. Then a few hours later the sun was going down and starting to become dark inside so I switched on my floor lamp and the bulb blew and popped at same time and glass flew out of the lamp in a whish as it popped.

`I thought, saying out loud, it's just a coincidence I will turn on the other lamps. I did and each one I turned on the bulbs blew, but not like you would expect, these blew but gave off a blew [blue] hew [hue] of light as they had blown. I thought, well, bad brand of bulbs and lit up some candles, I keep the fat ones around in case of power outages. I turn the tv on and the color keeps going all red to all green to all black and then the tv would shut off. I was freaking out just a bit but kept telling myself there was a plausible and reasonable explanation and not to get excited.

Then it happened, I started hearing someone, something, moan and speak in a foreign tongue and moan a bit, almost like you hear a mosque doing the evening prayer thing. I spoke to it and asked if it would speak to me in English because I don't understand your language. The room went quiet. I read eight chapters of a new book I had bought and then took a shower and went to bed.

I was awakened by the feeling of someone touching me on the cheek around 3 AM. I woke up quick and looked around and thought, *OMG, I am having a nightmare* and laughed it off. I went back to sleep and at 5 AM something grabbed my ankle and jerked it. I woke suddenly and fearful and thought, another nightmare but this time I had pressure fingerprints around my ankle. I have edema sometimes and if I cross my legs or rest them on something it leaves an impression. I was trying so hard to rationalize and then I realized I wasn't alone. I was sitting on the bed and began to feel weight all around me and fearful and I had a hard time moving like I was in cement. My body felt heavy and thick and like electricity was flowing through me but I couldn't seem to move and I kinda rocked left to right a bit and then it stopped.

Since this happened I have asked the seller to take it back and remove it from me and they sent me an email saying that I accepted it freely and now it was mine. I have not heard from them since then and it's been a few months. I have had several appliances blow up, I have had neighbors come to visit and bring their dog and have it look around the room like it sees something, whine and run out. Every time I take a picture in the house, when I get them developed they have little white spheres in the picture and sometimes you can see an image in the picture like a being but it is very small about the size of a doll.

I am plagued with odd smells and I have used plug-ins, Pinesol, Fabuloso, and Odo-ban and nothing seems to get rid of it. I have burned incense of myrrh or sandalwood and each time I light it, it goes out after a few seconds. No matter how well I light the incense it goes out. I have heard water running since I received the Djinn and I can't keep bread or milk without it ruining in a day or two.

Each day I get a new experience or incident. I have now begun to get door knocking at 1 AM. I hear someone knocking at the front door and I go turn on the light and go outside and no one is there. It doesn't repeat all night long it just happens once at 1 AM each night.

I paid 123 dollars for the Djinn on a website from India and if I ever knew that these things are for real I would never have bought it. The seller also told me that even if I destroyed the ring the Djinn is bound to me so it wouldn't matter, of course I wasn't informed of this until after it was shipped and I read it upon receipt. Nice huh...

For anyone ever thinking of buying online like this, please don't, I didn't believe and I wish I had never heard of a Djinn and it's like having a destructive roommate you can never see.

We have heard from other people who have bought "Djinn jewelry." Most such items have nothing attached to them, but others, like the case above, contain an entity that loves to create havoc. Some victims suffer severe problems, including nightmares and sexual assault. Once a negative spirit is attached to a person, an exorcism may be required to dislodge it. There are many kinds of exorcisms in various spiritual paths—not all of them are the formal demonic exorcisms performed in Catholicism, and popularized in horror films.

Is there such a thing as a dybbuk box?

In the early 2000s, a story about a haunted dybbuk box went through the paranormal community like wildfire. The "dibbuk box" (spelled with an i) was an old wooden wine cabinet supposedly purchased at an estate sale in Oregon in 2001. The back story was that it belonged to an old woman who had brought it with her from Europe, and instructed her family that it was never to be opened because it contained a dybbuk and a "keselim." The family seemed to think there was something evil or cursed about it, and sold it after the old woman died.

The man who bought it then suffered misfortunes that he attributed to the box. He sold it several years later on eBay to a group of college students who thought it was "cool" to own a haunted object. However, it seemed that anyone who came in contact with the mysterious box became ill or suffered misfortune.

The box was sold again on eBay to a Missouri man named Jason Haxton, who also experienced weird and negative phenomena. Haxton determined to get to the bottom of the mystery, and did extensive research to track down the true origins of the box. He opened the cabinet and found prayer stones inside, include a granite stone carved with the name of God.

Did the box contain a dybbuk, and if so, did that make it cursed?

What is a dybbuk?
In Jewish demonology, a dybbuk is an evil spirit or doomed soul that possesses a person body and soul, speaking through the person's mouth and causing such torment and anguish that another personality appears to manifest itself. The term *dybbuk* was coined in the seventeenth century from the language of German and Polish Jews. It is an abbreviation of two phrases: *dibbuk me-ru'ah* ("a cleavage of an evil spirit"), and *dibbuk min ha-hizonim* ("dibbuk from the demonic side" of man). Prior to the seventeeth century, the dybbuk was one of many evil spirits known as *ibbur*.

In early folklore, dybbukim (plural) were thought only to inhabit the bodies of sick persons, causing their illness. In the rabbinical literature of the first century, exorcisms called for the ashes of a red heifer, or the roots of certain herbs, burned under the victim, who was then surrounded with water. Other methods included incantations in the name of King Solomon, repetition of the Divine Name of God, reading from Psalms, and the wearing of herbal amulets.

By the sixteenth century, the concept of possessive evil spirits had changed. Many Jews believed the spirits were transmigrated souls who could not enter a new body because of their past sins, and so were forced to possess the body of a living sinner. The spirits were motivated to possess a body because they were tormented by other evil spirits if they did not. Some thought the dybbukim were the souls of people who were not properly buried, and thus became demons.

The Kabbalah contains rituals for exorcizing a dybbuk; many are still in use in modern times. The dybbuk either is redeemed or is cast into hell. It usually exits the body of its victim through the small toe, which shows a small, bloody hole as the point of departure.

More questions than answers

Both John and Rosemary had involvement with Haxton as his research unfolded, and consulted with him a number of times. Haxton was interested in writing a book about the box and was looking for a co-author. One prospective writer took on the project and then decided to drop out, citing unpleasant phenomena that had begun in his home, including the appearance of shadow people. Haxton then contacted Rosemary, who was interested in taking on the project. From the time of her first phone conversation with Haxton, she, too, had outbreaks of phenomena. One of the most pervasive was the strong odor of cat urine that permeated her condo. Rosemary owned no cats, nor did her neighbors. The cat urine smell even traveled with her as she went to distant locations.

By this time, the rights to the story had been sold to Hollywood, and a horror film was in production, produced by Sam Raimi (*The Evil Dead, Drag Me to Hell*, and numerous other film credits). Haxton wanted the book to coincide with the film release, but making that deadline was too short a time for Rosemary with her other commitments.

Haxton found another co-author, and released his book, *The Dibbuk Box*, in 2011. The film, delayed in production, was released in 2012 under the title *The Possession*.

In his book, Haxton came to two conclusions. One was that the box was "a genuine artifact of amazing power and magnetism," and had a mysterious power and mystical significance. The prayer stones inside acted as a focal point and battery for spiritual prayer. He believed there were ties between the box and the Holocaust. His second conclusion was contradictory: the box was a "fraud," its story fabricated for quick money-making purposes. Both of these assertions were true, he said.

In an afterword, Howard Schwartz states that there is essentially no such thing in Jewish practice as a "dibbuk box," a container for lost souls of sinners.

Significance of the box

If the dybbuk box was based on a false story, then why did so many people suffer genuine problems as a result of coming into contact with it? Why did so many people feel the box had an unsavory or evil feel to it?

Some of those effects probably can be explained as self-induced— if people believe an object is haunted and has the power to harm them, they may experience a wish fulfillment of that belief. However, not all of the wine cabinet's effects can be explained away so easily—not everyone affected had knowledge of the box's background.

One possibility—and this is our speculation—is that the box, which dates to the 1960s, at some point acquired an attachment of negative, unhappy human energy, or an attachment of a negative spirit. This energy might have influenced reactions to the box, including on the part of the individuals who were involved in creating the original back story.

Haxton's research and detective work alone make for a fascinating story, and certainly raise many questions about how and why some objects become afflicted.

7

The Burned Altar

The apartment was empty, save for a brooding presence that settled in while the occupants were away. The air, which had been peaceful and calm, took on an increasing feeling of pressure. It got tighter and heavier until, suddenly, the sacred altar burst into flames.

Larry and Debbie Elward arrived home to the pungent smell of smoke that filled their second floor apartment. There was no working fire, only the charred smell. At first, they were not alarmed. The landlady's son smoked while he made wine in the basement, and often the smell filtered up through their vents.

This smell, however, was far stronger. Debbie searched through the apartment looking for a cause. When she entered the spare bedroom, which was converted into their office and chapel, she shrieked.

"Larry! Look at this!"

Debbie and Larry could not believe their eyes. Their once tidy altar, filled with holy objects, was a fire disaster.

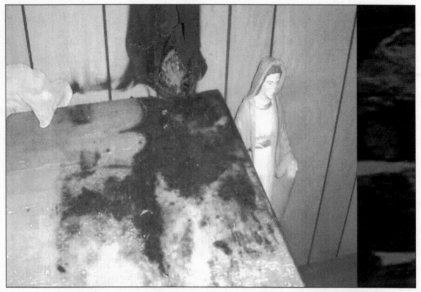

Charred altar top and scorched wall (Courtesy Debbie and Larry Elward)

Portions of the top of the wooden altar was charred black. The glass that had covered the top, and the white lace runner that had covered the glass, were missing. A pewter chalice had a gaping hole in it, as though shot through with a small missile. The plate atop it—the paten—was melted all over the sides of the chalice. One glass hobnail candlestick was gone, and all that remained of its matching one was a small, globby, misshapen ball. A relic of the Blessed Virgin Mary was scorched but intact, and it appeared that the path of the blaze had mysteriously gone around it. A prayer missal resting on a metal stand had its string bookmarks burned off, but otherwise was untouched. Not even the pages were singed.

The altar was only a few inches from a window, which had been left open. The sheer lace curtains, which could easily have caught fire, were untouched. A black char mark was on the wall.

It was a wonder that the entire place had not gone up in flames, but nothing else in the small room had been singed or burned. The fire appeared to have been confined to the altar—a weird version of spontaneous human combustion, in which fire consumes nearly an entire body, but barely burns anything around it. If this targeted fire was a message, Larry and Debbie understood it immediately—they had received a calling card from the Dark Side.

Melted chalice and paten (Courtesy Debbie and Larry Elward)

No strangers to the demonic

Larry and Debbie Elward meet the Dark Side head on almost daily in their spiritual work. For more than two decades, they have worked closely with John Zaffis on many cases of hauntings, attachments, infestations, and possession. They have brought relief to scores of victims, but that success comes with a price—the Dark Side fights back.

"We get a lot of warnings that demons or negative forces are put in our way to scare us away from helping people," said Debbie. "We never heed them, because we know that on the positive side, God is helping us."

Larry grew up in Bridgeport Connecticut. In 1973, he joined millions of people around the world who flocked into theaters to see *The Exorcist*, based on a true possession story, and full of horrific details the likes of which most of the general public had never before seen. The film awakened people to the reality—the *possibility*—of serious attack from powerful and evil forces.

John Zaffis, left, with Debbie and Larry Elward (Courtesy John Zaffis)

The film inspired Larry to become involved in paranormal work, especially from a religious and spiritual perspective. He became an investigator with Ed and Lorraine Warren in 1985 and worked on their famous case of the possession of Maurice Theriault, a tomato farmer in Warren, Massachusetts. Theriault had been abused by his father so badly that he called upon Satan for help. His deterioration led to significant problems and phenomena by the time he was in his late fifties, and the Warrens were summoned to the scene.

While working on this case, Larry witnessed his first demonic exorcism, performed by Bishop Robert McKenna, who was called in by the Warrens. It was quite an eye-opener on the powers of demonic forces. The case also brought him into contact with John, with whom he formed a lasting friendship that eventually led to a partnership in the Work, that is, fighting the forces of evil.

Larry entered religious training at the Holy Apostle Seminary, graduating in 1988 with a master's degree in theology. In 2002, he began studies in esoteric Christianity under Bishop Lewis Keizer of California. He was ordained a priest in 2004.

Larry and Debbie met at an exorcism in 1998. Debbie, a native of Watertown, Connecticut, was born with the biblical gift of discernment of spirits, and saw dead people at an early age. Her family was not enthusiastic about this gift, and dismissed it as an overactive imagination. There was no suppressing her ability, however, and as Debbie got older, she developed clairaudience as well, becoming able to hear and communicate with spirits as well as see them.

Larry and Debbie work as a team, on their own, with other investigators, and with John. They have had some strange and trying cases, and plenty of run-ins with negative entities.

The water poltergeist

There have been a number of cases from earlier centuries about "stone-throwing devils," invisible poltergeist agents who hurl stones about and cause them to manifest out of thin air inside houses. For example, in 1682 a household in New Castle, New Hampshire was plagued with mysterious rains of stones that fell from the sky onto the roof, and also materialized in the house, falling on the floor and furniture, and even clobbering people. The stones were of all sizes, and some were even hot to the touch. The attacks were believed to be diabolical in nature, and were blamed on a disagreeable neighbor suspected of being a witch. The stone rains stopped after a while, as suddenly as they had started.

The Elwards once encountered a *water* poltergeist—an unknown presence that cause water to rain down on people inside their home—gentler than stones, but nonetheless annoying and alarming.

The case concerned a family who owned two properties that were occupied year round. The grandmother lived in one of them, a cottage, by herself. One day, she was making pancakes in the kitchen, and rain started falling on her from inside the ceiling. Episodes of mystery rain increased—rain would fall inside the house on sunny days, primarily in the bathroom or kitchen. Water poured out of the ceiling in huge drops.

The second house also became infected, and rain poured out of ceilings there, too. The residents all were mystified. The poltergeist also moved around heavy furniture, such as an armoire in one of the bedrooms. The armoire was found relocated from its place along one wall to the center of the room. The parents at first suspected their daughter, a young girl, who vehemently denied moving it. She was a most unlikely culprit, anyway, for two adults were required to wrestle the armoire back into place.

Summoned for help, Larry and Debbie went out to the property and performed a house blessing. The family experienced gradual relief, with the phenomena decreasing over time and then ending.

The cause was never ascertained, though the Elwards suspected it had something to do with a resident spirit of the land. "We think something was awakened by human activity," said Debbie, "but we never found out exactly what it was. We lost touch with the family, which is not uncommon. Once people get help, it's sometimes too much of a strain to stay in contact. They don't want to keep being reminded of what they went through, and sometimes they are afraid that talking about it will make it come back."

Spirits of the land do act out against humans who come and occupy "their" territory, as we noted earlier. The faeries were famous in earlier times for bringing ruin to those who dared to trespass on or blight their territory—and they still do so in modern times. For example, since 2007, Icelanders trying to build a stretch of highway through a preserve said to belong to the elves have been stymied by all sorts of mishaps, accidents, and setbacks. Equipment keeps breaking down, and workers fall ill as well. To those who know the elves, this is no surprise. Humans, proceed at your own peril!

John and Rosemary have found similar elements in some of their cases—invisible residents that get riled up by people. Sometimes the entities remain dormant for long periods of time, and then start acting out when sufficiently energized. Reasons could be a change in human occupancy, or new activities on the property.

Curses

Larry and Debbie have dealt with more than a few curses in their cases. Usually a curse is put on someone by an ex-lover or ex-spouse, or a jealous lover in a triangle. Occasionally strange phenomena happen along with the torments of the victim, which include nightmares, unpleasant physical sensations, apparitions, disembodied voices, and poltergeist effects.

In one of their cases, a woman from Haiti was cursed by her ex-husband, using the magic of the island. She was in the United States and he was in Haiti with their children. The woman wanted to bring her children to the States, but the husband would have none of it, and had the curse placed on her.

It manifested in a sinister way. The woman began seeing a doppelganger of her ex in her house, and the doppelganger threatened her if she did not drop her efforts. She also was made to see an apparition of a god of death (perhaps Baron Samedi), with the threat that she would meet her end if she pursued seeing her children.

The Elwards prayed over the frightened woman and were able to break the curse.

In another case, the victim did not fare so well. A woman came to the Elwards for help, saying that her ex-lover had cursed her and was making her life miserable. She actually went blind, at least psychologically. Physically, there was nothing wrong with her eyes, yet she lost the ability to see. A powerful demon had been employed to carry out the curse. Debbie and Larry broke the hold of the demon, and the woman's sight returned. However, within three months, she was dead of hepatitis. Was she attacked again?

The Work has its hazards for both the victims and those who come to their aid. Like others in the field, the Elwards have had mishaps, runs of bad luck, accidents, and other circumstances that are "blowback"—the consequences of taking on the Dark Side.

The burning altar, which occurred in 2004, was only part of a string of mishaps and misfortunes that appeared to be attacks of something evil.

Run down

In 2003, both Larry and Debbie were run down by an elderly man at the wheel of a car. Larry was not expected to survive.

The incident happened one Sunday morning as Debbie and Larry departed church. Larry was dragged fifty feet and was run over three times: once by the rear wheels, then by the driver's wheel, then a third time by a front wheel. His broken body was dragged about fifty feet down the parish driveway and then thrown up on the lawn.

Debbie was hit and thrown. A third pedestrian, a woman, was struck as well and landed next to Debbie.

They were rushed to the hospital. Larry had extensive, life-threatening injuries: a broken nose, broken clavicle, bruised heart, all ribs broken in at least two places, a lung punctured by two broken ribs, pelvis broken in three places, a broken femur, broken finger, and a bruised diaphragm. Astonishingly, he was conscious throughout the entire ordeal and was beyond pain.

The doctors were not optimistic, and gave him a twenty percent chance of survival, adding that if he managed to survive, he probably would spend the rest of his life in a nursing home.

Debbie was treated at the hospital and released, but remained in unbearable pain. Something was wrong with her hip, but she was told at the hospital that it was just shock. She went home but could barely get around. She had to crawl on her hands and knees up the stairs to their second-floor apartment. It took her an hour to get into the car every time she went back to the hospital to visit Larry.

Larry miraculously improved overnight, to the point where doctors raised his odds of survival to fifty percent. He would not be defeated. On his third day in the hospital, his ventilator was removed. Two weeks to the day, he was released. He walked out and went home.

Both remained impaired and in considerable pain for a long time, and still feel the effects to this day. A year after the accident, doctors discovered that Debbie had broken her pelvis in two places. Over time, it healed reasonably well.

The accident was both foreseen and seen psychically by at least two people. One was a woman who had a dream of Larry being hit by a car. The other was a man from Georgia who did not know either Debbie or Larry, but called John on the day of the accident to ask him if he knew anything about an exorcist being run over by a car.

The Elwards received an insurance settlement but could not work for a long time. The driver had his license revoked but kept driving, and finally was arrested for not having a license or registration. At one point he coldly told the Elwards, "Even if you were family, I would not come to see you."

Discouraged, Debbie and Larry discussed whether or not they should continue the Work. This was a battering beyond anything they could have anticipated. Debbie was in favor of stopping and Larry was uncertain.

John helped them rally their spirits and their faith. "You have to continue," he told them. "Do you realize who saved you? God did!"

The Work goes on.

The altar aftermath

The burning altar was the first major attack on the Elwards since the accident, and it brought home the dangers of the Work in a new way. "It happened in our house, our safety place," said Debbie. This was an invasion of space that was supposed to be personal sanctuary.

Debbie and Larry cleaned up the damage. They increased their vigilance with regular prayer and house blessings, and maintaining shields of white light. Debbie keeps crystals in the windows to ward off negativity, and they use ample amounts of sea salt, also a deterrent. In addition, Larry uses holy medals and holy water, and Debbie draws upon her Shoshone heritage. "We cover all our bases," Debbie said.

Years later, they still marvel at the peculiar way the fire burned— or did not burn—on the altar. The prayer missal with its burned bookmarks but untouched pages was amazing, as was the relic of the Virgin Mary, a locket that contained a bit of her clothing. The fire had gone around the relic and left the glass intact, but oddly, there was a scorch mark on the wood beneath it. The locket had been used in many exorcisms, and had an effect on victims. When touched to the forehead, victims often shrieked, "Mary, no!"

Perhaps it exerts even more force now.

When John opened his Museum of the Paranormal, the Elwards gave him the altar, an example of what can happened when the Dark Side fights back.

8

Corrupted Religious Objects

When the forces of darkness attack, many people take refuge in their faith. It is the last barrier, the final defense, against the demonic. The representatives of that defense—holy objects, relics, statuary, medals, and so forth—are thought to be pure and untouchable by evil. Shocking it is, then, to find that the symbols of faith can be corrupted. They become weapons used for ill or become trophies of the dark forces, who demonstrate their power.

John's Museum of the Paranormal contains numerous religious items, including bibles, that became tainted with dark energy or attached by hostile presences.

The Virgin Mary's melted hands

John's first major demonic case was a polluted funeral home in Southington, Connecticut, a case made famous by Ed and Lorraine Warren in their book *In A Dark Place* (1992) written with Ray Garton, and turned into the film *The Haunting in Connecticut* (2009). It was there that John encountered a force of tremendous evil one night, an encounter that caused him to leave the case for several days.

The funeral home was rented in 1986 by Carmen and Al Snedeker, who had one daughter and three sons. The oldest son was suffering from Hodgkin's lymphoma, and was being treated at a University of Connecticut hospital. The Snedeckers moved from upstate New York to Southington to be closer to the hospital. The old house was inexpensive, but the Snedekers said no one ever told them in advance that it had been a funeral home.

The house had a creepy presence, but the family settled in. The equipment and paraphernalia of the former funeral home were still stored in the basement, which Carmen had not been able to see before renting the house because it was blocked by renovation materials. The son who was ill, Phillip, and his brother, Bradley, were given a bedroom in the basement. They slept in the casket display room, which was down the hall from the embalming room. Soon they started seeing terrifying apparitions and ghosts. Phenomena spread and affected the entire family. Lights went off and on without the benefit of light bulbs.

The funeral home had crucifixes nailed to eight door jambs, one on each side, a customary practice in a Catholic funeral home. These crosses were about three inches in height and made of brass, and had been firmly nailed into place for a long time, for the wood around the crucifixes had discolored with the gradual tarnishing of the brass.

As the demonic activity in the house increased, the crucifixes mysteriously disappeared, one by one. Carmen did not notice the disappearance until only four remained. She asked her children if they had taken them down, but they said no. This development was unsettling for Phillip, who said he would help Carmen search the house for them. They thought the crucifixes might have somehow been taken to the tool room, where much of the old funeral paraphernalia was still stored. They looked through every bin and found piles of head and toe tags, but no crucifixes.

The crucifixes were never to be found. Finally, only one remained. When it disappeared, all hell broke loose in the house. Carmen went looking for the crucifix and found only an empty place where it had been nailed to the wood. The stained outline of the crucifix was visible, but there was no indication that it—or any of the other crucifixes—had been pried off with tools, which would have been the only way a living person could have gotten them off of the walls.

Another item that went permanently missing—one deeply cherished by Carmen—was a rosary made of clear quartz beads, handmade especially for her by a blind woman at church. Carmen was only fourteen when she had purchased the rosary with her own money, the first item she had ever bought on her own. She had watched the woman work and admired her. All of the religious objects in the house went missing, but the rosary is still grieved by Carmen to this day.

The Snedekers contacted the Warrens, who began an investigation, with John assisting. According to Lorraine, the house had become polluted because of the activities that had gone on there while it was a funeral parlor, especially necrophilia performed by previous employees.

A twenty-four-hour-vigil was maintained by the investigators. At that point, the family members were all sleeping in the living room because they were too frightened to be in their bedrooms. One night when John was monitor, he encountered a gray reptilian form that came at him, muttering, "You know what they did to us." The form radiated a powerful evil energy. John grabbed his car keys and left the house in a hurry. He stayed away for three days while he debated whether or not to continue with the Work. He decided to return, because people like the Snedeckers need help in facing demonic forces. It was the first and only time John has ever reacted that way to an evil presence.

The Warrens asked Carmen to participate in a séance to see if she could communicate with the entity. Carmen reluctantly agreed. As the séance began, she prayed silently the Lord's Prayer, and also asked the angels for protection against any harm. She could feel the entity's evil all around her, and even could feel its breath. She could hear its voice in the air all around her. She was terrified, and kept up her intense inner praying.

The entity manifested. When she asked for its name, it replied, "I Am." It was a mocking of God. She asked for a name a second time, and it repeated, "I Am." To Carmen, it showed itself in a vision, jumping up on the table and ripping off the face of Ed Warren. Horrified, she rebuked the entity with her faith.

The séance was a trying experience for Carmen. The horrendous activity in the house continued. When it became apparent that house blessings and masses would not rid the house of the evil presence, the decision was made to conduct a formal exorcism, carried out by three priests and three deacons.

To prepare for their confrontation with the demon, the priests and deacons entered into a six-day "black fast" of purification, and were in the midst of it when they conducted the exorcism.

One of the deacons brought several religious items, including a statue of the Virgin Mary, which he placed on the fireplace mantle in the living room, and a statue of Jesus, nearly the same in size, which he placed elsewhere. The Madonna had her arms outstretched in a welcoming gesture, as though she was ready to hug someone.

The exorcism was carried out at noon in the dining room. It was performed three times, in Latin, English, and Hebrew. The demon reacted violently. The house rumbled and shook, and a supernatural light filled the room. The air grew tense and heavy. At one point, during the Gloria and the raising of the chalice, Ed clutched his chest and had to leave the room. He went out into a hallway, followed by Lorraine, and sat in a chair while the exorcism continued.

The exorcism expelled the demon who mockingly called itself "I Am," and suddenly the house felt clear. Everyone practically sagged with relief.

As the priests and deacons collected things and prepared to leave, Carmen talked with them about what to expect next. "When you are born, you are born into a room with no doors and windows," one of the priests said. "When the supernatural touches you, you now have a door. You can shut the door, but the door remains, and it can be reopened. If you are diligent, that will keep the door closed."

Carmen understood that she and the members of her family would have to remain vigilant for the rest of their lives to prevent the evil from returning. It was a sobering thought.

Carmen struck up a conversation with one of the deacons about relics while he collected the items he had brought into the house for the exorcism. She became distracted as the deacon walked into the living room to retrieve the Madonna. She turned around and found him frozen in place in front of the mantel, staring in disbelief at the statue. Sensing that something was dreadfully wrong, Carmen slowly approached the deacon.

"Look at the Madonna," he said in a strained voice.

Carmen looked and the statue and was shocked to see that Mary's hands were missing. They appeared to have been melted off—but there were no noticeable signs of fire, no puddles of melted wax on the mantel or floor. She reached out to touch the statue.

Virgin Mary with melted hands (Courtesy R.E. Guiley)

"Don't!" exclaimed the deacon.

Carmen quickly pulled her hand back. She looked at the deacon, who was still staring at the statue in disbelief. "Was it like that when you brought her in?" she asked.

"No! I would never use a non-intact religious article."

Not knowing what to do next, Carmen stood looking at the statue with the deacon. Abruptly, he turned and walked away.

"Are you just going to leave it?" Carmen called out after him.

The deacon stopped and turned around. "I can't touch it right now." He explained that because he was still in the fast, touching a defiled holy object would make him vulnerable to retribution by the demon that had just been exorcized. "I can come back for it later," he said. He indicated that he would dispose of the statue.

Carmen had been taught in her religious upbringing that one does not throw holy objects away. "I'll take care of her," she said.

For twenty years, Carmen cared for the mutilated statue, praying over it daily. She took it with her whenever she moved. She could not bring herself to get rid of it. When John opened his museum, she felt that it would be the perfect home for the statue, as well as serve as a lesson to others about the terrible powers of the Dark Side.

Since the exorcism, Carmen has remarried and returned to using her maiden name, Reed, professionally in the paranormal field. She has steadfastly maintained her "due diligence," her religious prayers and defenses against the demonic. "I check with God every day and keep my spiritual being cleansed as best as I can," said Carmen. "I always see God in everything. I know some people don't want to hear that—that that's what you have to do—but it's the truth."

Carmen acknowledged that there have been times when she has been concerned about a return of the evil. "Not with me, but with other people that he goes after, my children and my family. Some of them keep up their due diligence and some have not."

She also said that even talking about the case, including being interviewed for this book, sets off warning lights for her. "That being will hover just out of his reach for me and my reach for him, letting me know that he is there," she said.

Rosemary and Carmen had an odd experience during the writing of this book. Rosemary interviewed Carmen, and they did not have further communication for several weeks. Rosemary worked on the chapter late one night, and was well into the early morning hours when she stopped.

The next morning when she arose, Rosemary found a message from Carmen waiting for her. "I woke up with this on my mind," Carmen said. She added a lengthy text with more details about the incident.

Had Rosemary and Carmen exchanged a telepathic connection during the night—or had a watching entity tapped her on the shoulder as Rosemary worked?

Once you come face to face with evil, it is always there, looking in from the other side of the window glass.

Cursing with Jesus

Holy objects can become corrupted by humans as well as entities. John has in his museum a large statue of Jesus with his sacred heart showing, which was used to curse people.

The Jesus statue was one of several religious objects used by a woman to put spells on people she did not like. Her written spells, along with the victims' names, were taped to the undersides of each object. Some of the victim became ill and some may even have died.

Jesus statue used for curses (Courtesy John Zaffis)

John did a binding on the statue and placed it in the museum. From time to time, small puddles of an oily fluid were found at the base of the statue, as though it had been weeping.

How could a religious object—in this case of the Son of God—be used to bring harm to people?

"Any religious item that has a lot of meaning to someone can be used to hide negativity," John explained.

Throughout history, figures of gods, angels, and saints have been used to lend power to curses. In such cases, the curse probably takes the form of a negative prayer: praying to Jesus, for example, to bring down a perceived enemy. Some may believe that praying against a person is acceptable—after all, they feel they are in the right—but it is the same as cursing. Prayer is a power, a force, an act of calling on a higher power for aid. The purpose of that aid is determined by the person who is praying. The power of prayer can be used for or against anything.

Writing down a spell and then placing it beneath a religious object such as a statue is an aid in manifesting the spell.

John has many religious and holy statues and objects in his museum that have been used for harm. Perhaps the perpetrators do not realize that the greatest harm they do is to themselves, in a different kind of blowback, for what you send out, you get back.

9

The Thing in the Stone Egg

It was a curious but innocent-looking polished stone egg—but it packed a powerful supernatural punch that knocked paranormal researcher Justin Spurrier for the terrifying loop of his life.

Justin discovered the stone egg as he sifted through the belongings of a vacated home that he purchased for his family in Kansas. It was interesting and cool, and Justin decided to keep it.

The house had belonged to a Hispanic family who had moved to the area from Mexico in the late 1930s. The husband and wife lived in the house until they died. One day in 1994, the husband prepared to do home repairs, and was walking out the door with a bag of concrete mix and a shovel. Suddenly, he collapsed from a massive heart attack and died on the spot.

His wife lived another ten years in the house before passing away in 2004. She kept everything the same as it had been while her husband was alive—including leaving his boots beside the door. The house was, in a way, a death shrine.

After her death, the house passed to their children, who allowed it to become even more of a macabre memorial, leaving it exactly as it had been left by their mother. The house remained empty of people for years, with nothing but ghosts to enjoy the furnishings and personal belongings. The bills were paid and the house was regularly cleaned, as if the parents were still alive.

Finally, the financial burden became too much, and the children put the house up for sale, including everything in the house. Justin purchased it in 2014. He did not really want the furnishings, but the principal daughter who was handling the sale did not want to take anything away. Perhaps she feared that everything in the house might be cursed in some strange way by the deaths of her parents, and the fact that a "ghost house" had been maintained for so long.

Something paranormal or supernatural had indeed been resident in the house, or at least in the minds of the previous owners. All the walls were covered with religious artifacts and items. Every doorway was guarded by a cross. Some of the crosses were mere pieces of straw that had been bent into shape. A great deal of holy water was on the premises. Had the family had to ward off some evil presence?

Justin contacted the surviving family members, but no one wanted anything from the house. So, he began inspecting all the belongings, looking for items he wanted to keep. He started moving many things out. He wanted to clear the house for his family to move in.

Justin came across the polished stone egg in a drawer. The egg was large, filling his hand. It was smooth and polished, with a beautiful grained look of reds and oranges with a little white mixed in. One side of it was brighter in color than the other. He wondered if it was supposed to have a stand for display, but if so, the stand was missing.

My kids would like this, Justin thought to himself, and tucked it with other items he had decided to keep.

Justin made no attempt to research the stone egg with the family—something he regretted later—and took it home. A warning of caution prompted him to leave the egg in a bag on the porch and not take it into the house.

There the stone egg sat, forgotten for three months. Justin did not remember the egg until the day he bought a rock tumbler for his kids. It normally takes a long time to polish stones in a tumbler—weeks to months. Justin got an idea to play a little trick on the kids. The next morning, he fished out the stone egg and showed it to them, telling them it had been polished overnight. Then he admitted that he was just teasing.

That evening, Justin and his wife, Audrey, put the children to bed and then turned in early themselves, around 9 PM. Justin casually tossed the stone egg into the sock drawer of his dresser, which was about ten feet away from the head of the bed.

Shortly before midnight, he came suddenly awake, just in time to see a black, streaky mass about five to six inches wide shoot out of the closed sock drawer straight up into the air and then hurtle at him. The mass turned into a violent swirling cloud of smoky mist in multiple shades of gray. The swirling mist expanded and kept coming closer and closer, until it took up the entire field of Justin's vision. A rumbling, growling sound filled the air.

What the--? Justin thought to himself, tightening in alarm.

He was just about to waken his sleeping wife when he was abruptly yanked up off the bed and suspended in air. His back was arched at a sharp angle about a foot off the bed, and his shoulders and feet were several inches up. Justin was paralyzed, unable to move a muscle or even cry out. He felt as if he were watching himself in a horror film.

Then a force seized hold of him and began to crush him. It felt like a giant python wrapped around his chest, squeezing all the air out of him. Every breath got shorter and shorter. His eyes blinked in strobe-like fashion, way too fast. The Thing that gripped him snarled and growled.

Justin could not turn his head, but he could see his wife out of the corner of his eye. Why wasn't Audrey waking up? How could she sleep through this horror? *Audrey, please wake up! Please wake up!* Justin screamed silently.

The Thing kept choking him as he floated above the bed. He summoned his energy and said silently, as forcefully as he could muster, *I command you in the name of God to let me go!*

Normally, he would have used "Jesus," but somehow it came out spontaneously as "God."

Nothing happened! The Thing continued its iron grip on Justin's body.

Then Audrey rolled over in her sleep and the force broke. The Thing released Justin and slammed him down on the bed. Audrey woke up to see Justin gasping and stuttering. She never got a glimpse of the mass that had formed in the room. It vanished.

When Justin got his breath, he told Audrey what had happened. Even though he had been physically pummeled and squeezed, there was not a mark or bruise upon his body.

Justin was so rattled that he could not let the matter rest until morning. Whatever had come out of the stone egg was dark and possibly demonic, and had to be dealt with immediately. He got on the phone and contacted several friends. Usually, Justin was the go-to guy for paranormal issues, but now he was the one in need of emergency help. He was referred to a priest in Texas. The priest answered the phone, even though it was the middle of the night.

Justin put the priest on speaker phone and prayed while the priest prayed over him. The priest then instructed Justin on how to banish the Thing back into the stone egg with verbal commands and visualizations. The two of them worked through the process together. It took all of Justin's energy and inner strength, but at last he could feel a force being pushed back into the stone egg.

He went immediately outside and buried the stone in his backyard. He got out a sage bundle and burned it throughout the house to cleanse it. The entire process took several hours.

Justin was uneasy for days, waiting to see if the Thing escaped its grave and returned. Evidently, it had been successfully forced back into the stone egg, which now was imprisoned in the earth.

For a couple of nights, Justin had a difficult time sleeping, and tossed and turned restlessly. When it appeared that there would be no immediate blowback, his anxiety eased and he felt clear.

Then, much to Justin's horror, his dog was magnetized to the burial spot, and every day dug up the stone egg. Justin kept reburying it, fearing the Thing would get loose again. After a week of the dog unearthing the stone, Justin created a tombstone of bricks over the top of the stone's grave. The dog busily pushed all the bricks out of the way and once again dug up the stone. Justin got bigger, heavier bricks. Finally, the dog was thwarted, and left the stone egg alone.

Justin was still unsettled about the stone egg. He did research to try to learn what exactly the stone egg was, and what inhabited it. He turned up few leads. The stone may have been used in a magical way to absorb negative energy—or perhaps bad spirits had even been cast into it. The stone may have trapped bad spirits or energy for a long time, until Justin jostled it loose by handling it. Clearly, the family had worried about keeping negative forces at bay, given the festooning of crosses and religious items all over the house.

Justin continued to clear out the new house. He found a stash of old family photos, and got in touch again with members of the family of the previous owners. Yes, they wanted the photos! Then he brought up the stone egg, and suddenly the conversation chilled. No, none of them knew a thing about it. Justin told them what had happened. Suddenly, the family members no longer wanted the photos. They did not want anything that had been inside the house. Throw the photos away, they told Justin. Get rid of them!

Justin kept a few more of the artifacts he found in the new home, but none of them gave him any trouble. The dog left the burial spot alone. That status quo remained until Justin and his family moved, and a friend rented the old house. The friend who rented it knew about the stone egg and its burial location. Fortunately, his dog left the spot alone. There were no more no paranormal difficulties in the house.

Justin took his experience as both a warning and a blessing. "It was a wakeup call," he told John and Rosemary. "I've deal a lot with lower entities, like imps. This experience let me know that there are things out there that are far more powerful, and I need to have my guard up. It renewed my faith as well."

Ideally, the egg should have been buried in a distant location where it was unlikely to be disturbed, but Justin did do the right thing by putting it underground. His experience illustrates that one can never underestimate dark energy, and never be too careful. Every researcher in the field is blind-sided at one time or another.

10

The Enchanted Walking Stick

Many people search for a way to stay young, or turn back the clock and be young again. But how about a supernatural treasure that sends a person into fast-forward aging—as well as into some supernatural twilight zone?

At seventeen, Jack had plenty of years to spare before growing old. Advanced age is one of the last things on a teen's mind, something that will happen in a dim and distant future—and surely only to others.

For a teen, Jack had a peculiar interest in old things, however, and he loved to prowl the junk and estate shops in his New England area, handling objects of eras gone by, worlds that no longer existed. Occasionally he would buy something, but most of the time he just liked to handle them, as if touching them could open the door to another time.

One day, Jack got his subconscious wish—only the door was not to the past, but to the future.

He was strolling by one of his favorite shops and stopped to peer into the window. He had just been inside a day or two before, so it was unlikely that there was anything new—but some inner urge prompted him to look in.

Wow! Something caught his eye. Excited, he hurried inside.

The item that had beckoned to him was an old fashioned walking stick. It appeared to be hand-carved and was smooth and shiny. It practically jumped into his hand. Jack was particularly drawn to strange symbols that had been carved on the shaft. He had no idea what they meant, but he was certain they were occult, and they lent the stick an exotic air. He stabbed the stick onto the floor and leaned on it.

The price tag read twenty-five dollars, more money than he had on him. He checked his pockets and found only a ten-dollar bill.

Jack took the stick up to the counter where a bespectacled, older man was rummaging through drawers behind the counter. He was not the owner, the usual guy Jack saw. Jack's heart sank. This man might not give him a deal like the owner usually did.

The man looked up at him. His horn-rimmed glasses made him look like an owl. "Can I help you?" he said.

"Uh, is, uh, Mr. Granger here?" Jack stammered. Maybe the owner was in the back.

Owl man shook his head. "Nope. Not today." He eyed the walking stick in Jack's hand. "You want that?"

"Yeah, but..." Jack's voice faded as he handed over the stick.

The man looked at the price tag. "That'll be twenty-five dollars."

"Well, I haven't got twenty-five dollars. I was wondering if you would take ten?" Jack paused. "That's all I've got."

"Ten! I can't come down that much. Ten percent, maybe, but not more than half. Granger would have a fit. This just came in." He shoved the price tag at Jack so that he could see the date written on it. Jack knew that items were dated when they were put out for sale, and things that sat unsold for a long time were more likely to be heavily discounted. The walking stick had arrived in the shop the day before.

Jack looked crestfallen. He had to have this weird stick with the odd symbols. He didn't know why, but he had to have it. He had never seen anything like it before. It was not going to happen, however. Thoughts of cajoling and pleading ran through his mind, but after glancing at the stone face of owl man, he let the idea go.

He started to turn to leave when owl man exclaimed, "Oh, all right! Take it." He thrust the stick at Jack.

Jack grinned and pulled out his ten-dollar bill. This was his lucky day!

Owl man mumbled unintelligibly to himself as he completed the sale on the register. He pushed a receipt across the counter to Jack. "Enjoy yourself," he said, without looking at him.

Jack was delighted. He used the stick as he walked home, poling it along on the ground like he was a grand duke. The stick had a strange energy. Jack thought he felt something like an electrical charge run up the stick into his hand when he pushed the tip onto the ground.

At home, he marveled at his prize, wondering what the symbols meant. Were they for some magical ritual? Who had carved them onto the stick, and why? Some Gandalf-like guy?

Jack intended to research the symbols to find out what they meant, but that was a lot of effort, and he kept getting distracted. He kept the stick by his bed and liked to handle it every now and then, fantasies of being in charge of magical rituals running through his head.

Bizarre dreams started on the very first night the stick was in the house, and repeated almost every night. In the dreams, Jack saw a white-haired old man, his face lined with deep creases. He was bent over and misshapen, and his hands were spotted and gnarled with the effects of arthritis and age. Jack awakened with the strange feeling that *he* was the old man in the dreams.

Jack was the kind of person who was instantly fully awake in the morning, and could spring out of bed and straight into action—not like some of his friends who woke up groggy and moving in slow-motion. Now some odd force seemed to take him over. The dreams sucked out all his energy, and he woke up feeling exhausted. It was more than being merely tired, however. He felt, well, *old*.

As the days wore on, Jack could not shake the feeling that he was getting older by the minute. When he looked at himself in the mirror, he swore he actually looked older, especially in the face. He started moving more slowly, his body wracked with unusual aches and pains. In the mornings, he felt crippled and stiff, as though his body were fossilizing.

Jack liked to take the walking stick to school to show it off, and soon he was leaning on it more than ever. His friends poked fun at him as he shuffled along the halls, bent over like an old man. They thought he was faking it, but it was all too real for Jack.

He slacked off in his studies, unable to concentrate in class. He kept falling asleep, especially in the afternoons. His physical education teacher could not understand why Jack wanted to drop out of track—and why the walking stick was so important to him.

Jack had a part-time job after school and on weekends, working at a hardware store. His boss had always appreciated his good attitude and his attentiveness to customers. Like the teachers at school, the boss was puzzled and then alarmed by the rapid changes he saw in Jack. He wondered if the youth was sick, or perhaps had other problems.

Jack started avoiding his friends. Instead of hanging out with his buddies, he begged off. He had a new fondness for going off into the woods alone, with his walking stick, where he took long hikes. Walking was now difficult for him, but he felt compelled to take these walks. As he limped along surrounded by trees and the sounds of nature, he felt himself spinning off beyond his body, transported to other places in time. He felt as old as the hills, and in possession of some secret knowledge that he could not articulate.

The school counselor called Jack in for a chat. Teachers had noticed a change in his behavior and performance—was there anything he would like to talk about? Was he having difficulty at home? Was he in trouble of any kind? Jack sat bent over in his chair, as though he could not straighten his spine, a smile frozen on his face. No, he insisted, everything was fine.

What was that stick he kept with him, the counselor wanted to know. Why was it so important? Just a cool thing he found in a shop, Jack replied. The counselor noted the symbols—what did they mean? He shrugged and smiled.

Jack's parents, Bob and Marianne, became quite concerned about the changes in Jack's demeanor and behavior. At first, they thought it was an affectation that would wear off in its novelty. The changes worsened—and then the school officials called, voicing similar concerns.

Bob and Marianne confronted Jack, who kept a frozen smile on his face and shrugged. He had no explanation, and denied that anything was wrong. He kept his walking stick planted in front of him as he spoke.

"What's with this stick?" Bob wanted to know. "You cart that thing around with you everywhere."

"It's a cool stick, I found it in a shop," Jack said. He shrugged again. "I just like it."

Bob and Marianne exchanged puzzled looks.

Jack's parents talked in private. They ruled out drugs. Jack had never shown any interest in drugs, nor did he hang out with users at school.

Bob wanted to send Jack to a psychiatrist.

Marianne resisted. "I can't help but think that this walking stick of his has something to do with this," she said. "Everything started after he brought that thing home. And he won't be separated from it, like it has some sort of hold on him."

Bob made a sound of disagreement. "What could that have to do with anything? It's a stick! There's something else going on." He stabbed a finger at his head.

Marianne prevailed. She took the stick away from Jack and hid it under her bed. Jack improved a bit. He started walking straighter, though was still bent, and he seemed to have more energy. He was still lost in an internal world, however, remote and inaccessible to his parents. The bizarre dreams had stopped, and Jack missed them, but said nothing, except to complain about not having his stick.

The dreams may have stopped for Jack, but instead, his mother got them. She had no idea that her son had been having weird dreams, but now she was having the same ones, of seeing a strange, white-haired old man, decrepit with age and leaning on a walking stick. The dreams were accompanied by the unexplainable feeling that *she* was the old man. Marianne awakened from sleep feeling achy and old, with strange electrical-like pulses running through her body.

After the dream repeated several times, Marianne knew that something was indeed wrong—these were not one-off dreams of her own. She had paid attention to her dreams throughout much of her life, and knew when dreams were not "ordinary." What was more, she was starting to feel like an outside force or personality was asserting itself on her, as though it were trying to take her over.

Marianne did not share her thoughts with her husband. He completely rejected the idea of anything paranormal, and would not understand. Quietly, she took to the internet to see if she could find information that would explain what was going on. When she found the website of John Zaffis, she instinctively knew that he was the right person to contact.

John arranged an appointment at their home at a time when he could speak with both Marianne and Jack. He questioned Jack at length, looking for signs of involvement in the occult, such as performing magical rites, using a spirit board, or reading books about summoning. Jack denied it, and John could tell from his demeanor that the young man was not hiding anything. Nonetheless, just to be certain, John asked for permission to do a walk-through of the house. He inspected every room, and found no images, statues, books, tools, or other objects associated with occult rites.

The walking stick was still hidden beneath Marianne's bed. John prompted Jack to talk about the stick.

Jack was unwilling to say much—it was his private little secret, and he didn't want to let the world in on it. He described finding the stick and being drawn to it. He admitted that when his mother had taken the stick away from him, he felt as though some sort of energy on hold on him had been broken. As he talked, Marianne became increasingly agitated.

Suddenly she shouted, "I want that stick out of the house! It's the cause of all these problems!"

Jack was upset and his face twisted into an angry expression. "I don't have it, you know that!" he shouted back. "I don't know where it is, but I want it back!" He jumped up and stormed out of the house, slamming the back door. Moments later, Marianne and John heard the sound of a car engine, and then a car backing out of the drive and peeling down the street. Jack had gone off in the car his father had bought him for his sixteenth birthday.

Marianne looked helplessly at John. Without a word, she rose up and went off to the bedroom, and returned minutes later with the walking stick. She handed it to John, and he motioned her to set it down on the floor.

Marianne told him about her own dreams and strange sensations after she had put the walking stick under her bed. As she got worse, Jack seemed to improve. "Is it—possessed?" she asked.

John looked at the symbols, recognizing many of them. Whoever had owned this walking stick was knowledgeable about the occult, and about summoning. "It has an attachment," he said. "Possibly a combination of things. The owner was into magic and summoning, which attracted a lot of spirits to him, and one or more of them probably attached to him. There's something of the owner in the stick as well." John explained to Marianne the concept of residual energy, how people can leave powerful imprints on their personal possessions that can linger and even affect others. Not everyone who comes into contact with infected items is affected. John said, pointing out that Bob had evidently been immune to the stick.

Marianne looked uneasy. "But Jack—is he...permanently affected, like possessed? What about me?"

"The effects are usually temporary," John said. "As long as the object is around, it can have an effect on people who are around it." He did not mention that in some cases, the spirit is able to leave the object and latch on to something else, even a person. No need to plant the worry for something that may not happen. It was too early to tell what the lingering problems might be.

"What about the dreams?" she asked.

"The dreams may have reconnected you and Jack to the owner— that would be part of the residual energy. It might have gotten help from a spirit attachment, too. The energy was so strong that you both started taking on the physical characteristics of the owner, who evidently was an old man. Do you know anything about its history?"

Marianne shook her head.

John nodded. "Most of the time, no one knows the background of an item—they just are attracted to it, even magnetized. The spirit attached to an object might be looking for a new source of energy."

Marianne shivered. "Are we—me and Jack—attached in any way now?"

"It's too early to say, but I'm going to take care of this right now," said John. He pulled out small vials and proceeded to treat the stick with salt and holy water, silently saying binding prayers over the walking stick.

"You should keep this out of the house," John said when he was done.

Marianne put out her hands as though to push the walking stick away. "I don't want it anywhere near here! Can you take it away and throw it out?"

"I'll take it and put it where it will be safe and not bother anyone," John said. "Throwing it away could enable someone to pick it up and have the same problems."

"I don't care," said Marianne, "as long as it is out of *this* house."

John removed the walking stick and took it home. He left it out in the sunlight and then treated it again with salt, holy water, and binding prayers. The walking stick now resides in the museum.

Was the spirit attached to the stick evil? Problematic and harmful would be better descriptions. There was residual energy attached to the stick in the form of a shell from the previous owner, who probably was deceased. The shell was inhabited by a spirit, perhaps one that had attached to him during magical rituals. The spirit was keeping the shell personality alive, which had a detrimental effect on two people to come into contact with it, Jack and Marianne. Had the stick remained in the household long enough, Bob may have eventually come under its baleful field.

Objects that have been used for occult purposes are resold all the time, in shops and on the internet. Before acquiring them, research their history as much as possible, and determine the meaning of any symbols carved on them. If unusual effects manifest physically or mentally, put the object out of the house, and find help.

11

Hudson Valley Havoc

Earlier we described how people who live in portal areas have to deal with daily, often intense levels of paranormal phenomena. For some, the experience proves to be overwhelming, and they have to get out. Others suffer through a host of problems, including marital, financial, and health as well as paranormal. What happens to portal residents, and how do they cope—or not? The Hudson Valley has many cases that Rosemary and John have investigated over the years. One of them stands out as a haunting in the extreme.

The House on Mayhem Road

Lynn and Jim never intended to buy a house in the northern reaches of the Hudson Valley countryside. They were an engaged couple on the hunt for a new home, and were concentrating their search close to New York City, where they lived. One day, they were out driving around in in the countryside and passed an imposing house with a "For Sale" sign out front. Something about the place beckoned to Lynn, and she felt inexplicably drawn to it. However, their real estate agent refused to show it to them, saying only, "That house is not for you."

They should have listened and kept on looking. Instead, Lynn found another agent and insisted on seeing the property. When she at last set foot on the property, she was hooked, and paid no mind to important red flags. Despite an overheated real estate market in which houses in the area were quickly selling at asking prices and higher, this house had sat vacant for some time, and the price was well below market value. Lynn didn't care why—she just wanted the house, and no other would do. Soon, it was theirs.

At first glance, the place was indeed attractive. The house was well set back from a pleasant, winding road, with wild, pastoral acreage behind it. In the distance, trees glistened on hillsides. It seemed an ideal country retreat, a genteel home with an antique feel. Lynn envisioned warm summer nights on the spectacular patio, and cozy winter nights inside.

But the peaceful patina was false, for underneath seethed a writhing, paranormal presence just waiting for the next victims to move in.

Mayhem was about to break.

All stirred up

After moving in, Lynn and Jim undertook major renovations. Construction and remodeling often stir up activity in a haunted location. However, when a house sits in an active portal—like this one—the activity is high to begin with, and when stirred up even more, it does not die down.

Right away, things at Mayhem Road constantly went wrong. Not the usual contractor glitches, but odd things. The couple would come home and find the heat on up to 90 degrees, or else off altogether, including the furnace burner. New smoke alarms were installed and wired to a home protection security company. If the fire or door alarms went off by accident, a phone call had to be placed between the home and security provider to prevent the dispatch of the local police or fire departments. Too many false alarms would result in fines.

As soon as they were installed, the smoke alarms started going off by themselves between 3-5 AM. The security company would call for verification—but the house phone line inexplicably would go dead, and so the fire department would be contacted and dispatched. After several of these incidents, including one night in which the fire department responded twice, Jim disconnected the alarms and took out the batteries. The alarms went off, anyway—but at least they were no longer connected to the security company, and the fire department was not summoned. The sound of an alarm even went off in the attic, though no alarm was installed there.

Jim set up his office in a small building outside the main house. One window commanded a sweeping view of the back property. One day, his eyeglasses went missing. He searched his office and the main house, but they had simply vanished. A few days later, he glanced out his office window. His glasses were perched high in the branches of a tree right in back of the building. They looked carefully arranged, as though someone—or some *thing*—had placed them intending for him to see them.

Another time, Jim decided to take a break from work and catch some sun on the patio. He took his watch and wedding ring off and set them down on his desk with the watch encircling the ring. Then he went outside. When he returned to his office, the watch was on the desk, but his wedding ring was gone. Unlike the eyeglasses, it never returned.

The atmosphere in the home always seemed unsettled and even uninviting. The couple was subjected to a constant barrage of activity in and around the house. Weird popping noises sounded, especially when Lynn walked into the kitchen. Loud banging sounds emanated from empty rooms. Phone calls were plagued by loud buzzing and grinding noises; sometimes the phones did not work at all. Sometimes Lynn heard what sounded like the kitchen door opening and shutting with a loud bang, though no one ever entered the house. There were odd flashes of blue lights in the house and outside. The flashes often preceded phenomena, such as footsteps in the hallway and up and down the stairs.

Neither of them slept well at night. A growling sound could be heard in the hall. Green and red lights bobbed around outside the windows. The sounds of people talking in other rooms kept disturbing them, and almost nightly heavy footsteps came down the hall toward their bedroom. Sometimes Lynn heard the bedroom door open. Occasionally she had attacks, as though an invisible weight was pressing down on her. She had the sensation once of a man on top of her, trying to insert something into the roof of her mouth. She was frequently exhausted from the constant nighttime disturbances—and then had to deal with more during the day.

Foul septic-like smells spilled out of closets without explanation. Foggy forms and shadow people of varying sizes darted around in the house and showed up in a mirror in the dining room. One day following a major electrical storm, Lynn saw what appeared to be a man in a black suit walk past the front of the house. She and Jim went outside to investigate, but he had disappeared. Lynn decided to fetch a book from her car, and continued to the parking area while Jim returned to the house. He seemed nervous and wanted her to come inside as soon as possible. As she got to her car, Lynn spied the black-suited man walking out in the field behind the house, heading toward the woods. She took off after him. She had to know who he was, and why he was on their land. Suddenly she saw the apparition of her dead father in front of her. His voice came into her head: *Get back in the house now!*

A weird, electrical surge slammed through her body, and the next thing Lynn knew, she was lying on the ground being revived. She learned that a lightning bolt had struck and felled a tree across the street, and she had been hit by shock waves traveling through the ground.

The black-suited man was not the only presence to walk around the house and the field in the back. Lynn also saw the apparition of a woman there, as well as a large black mystery cat. It was too big for a domestic cat and not quite as big as a panther or jungle cat—and was not quite a cat, either, but something more "cat-like." It prowled around in the tall grass and then vanished.

The bedroom disturbances became so severe that Lynn often could not sleep through the night. Besides the footsteps, flashing lights, sounds, weights, and surgically-minded presences, there was something that liked to shake and damage the bed. The shaking felt like someone pushing the bed from the foot, and also as though someone had their hands beneath the mattress, trying to flip it up. Once Lynn awakened with her nightclothes turned inside out. The bottom bed sheet was ripped straight down the middle, as though someone had taken a razor to it.

Some of the presences were vague, but the apparitions of the old man and the woman stood out. Lynn felt they had strong ties to the house. Perhaps they had lived there, or even died there.

The dirt floor basement was especially creepy. Lynn hated to go downstairs to do the laundry because she always felt watched. One day she was alone in the house and went downstairs to start a load of laundry. While she was at the washing machine, the door at the top of the stairs suddenly slammed shut by itself. Alarmed, Lynn dashed upstairs, thinking an intruder might be in the house. When she tried to open the door, she could not—it was locked and could not be budged. She had no phone available and Jim was away for the day.

Lynn fought down panic and kept tugging on the door, now aware of a heavy, oppressive presence permeating the basement. Just when her panic reached a heart-stopping pitch, the door sprang open of its own accord.

Even their dog, a mastiff named Lucy, was affected by the house. Lucy was frequently in a state of agitation, on alert, panting heavily, and reluctant to go into certain parts of the house.

A lunar connection

After a few months of unrelenting unease mixed with fright and abject terror, Lynn noticed that the phenomena followed certain patterns. Activity was heavy at the new moon and at the full moon. On other nights, she could tell when things would be bad because the atmosphere would change and acquire a queer, almost electrical feel. The wild animals acted strangely. If the coyotes and the owls "talked" to each other in certain ways at the onset of darkness, Lynn knew that they were in for a horrible night.

The lunar phase synchronicity occurs throughout paranormal phenomena. The full moon has always been the "witching time," a time when supernatural and nighttime powers are at their peak. Full moons have been linked to increases in crime, accidents and, literally, lunacy, or madness. The full moon is associated with the psychic faculty as well. These associations, along with folklore beliefs that have grown up around them, have been documented for centuries. One reason that may account for the lunar connection is that the moon rules the tides, and the natural world and the human body are largely watery in nature. In the ancient view, planetary bodies such as the moon influenced the internal fluids, or "humors," of the body. Whatever the reason, anyone who spends much time in paranormal work soon notices that phenomena spike around the full moon.

The new moon, often overlooked in the paranormal field, has the same effect, and sometimes even a greater effect. In folklore and magic, the new moon is a dangerous time, and is ideal for the performance of black magic and "undoing" spells.

Lynn noticed a stronger increase in phenomena around the new moon than the full moon. The peak periods would cover one to two days before and after a new moon, and sometimes the same for a full moon. "I didn't even need to look up the phase on a calendar," Lynn said. "I could tell by a change in the activity."

These unsettled periods were marked not only by an increase in activity but also a change in the nature of the activity. It was difficult for Lynn to describe, other than there was a marked shift in "atmosphere" and "vibe."

Strung out

Lynn consulted local ghost investigators, hoping to find explanations for the persistent activity and get solutions to get rid of it, but no one could offer any suggestions that helped on an enduring basis. Her doctor of oriental medicine, whom she consulted for acupuncture and medical qi gong treatments, assured her that she had no spirit attachments.

At one point, Lynn contacted a famous medium who was a consultant to a major television show. She offered to bring the medium out from California to assess their situation. After hearing the details about the activity at the house, the medium declined, and instead told her to "write a letter to the ghosts" asking them to leave. Lynn should do this at a time when a local funeral parlor was having services. Apparently matching the letter writing to the funeral services was supposed to be conducive to the spirits to leave, at least according to the medium.

Lynn was so desperate that she was willing to try anything, so she followed through, but felt silly calling up a funeral home and then writing a letter to the invisibles with a "pretty please leave us alone" request. It did not work. In fact, nothing she tried worked.

By the time Lynn found Rosemary, she and Jim had lived in the house for about two years. Hanging on by their fingernails might be a more apt description, for they were at wit's end trying to cope with phenomena that frightened them and was beyond their comprehension, and would not desist. Lynn was profoundly physically drained, and was suffering from vertigo and insomnia. Her hair was falling out from stress. She and Jim were constantly on edge, and fought and bickered over inconsequential things.

Rosemary noted that Lynn and Jim lived in a particularly "hot" area of the Hudson Valley. The entire stretch of the Hudson River and its environs in New York State has a long history of hauntings, faeries and "little people," mysterious creatures and phenomena, and, since the mid-1980s, a great deal of UFO activity. A famous wave of black triangle ships in the sky had been witnessed by thousands of person for several years in the mid-1980s. The wave had even drawn the attention of the famous UFO debunker, J. Allen Hynek.

Even knowing the history of the area, Rosemary was still surprised at the intensity, variety, and persistence of paranormal phenomena that was taking place on the property. She dubbed the place "The House on Mayhem Road."

Investigations begin

The first investigation day was scheduled as soon as possible, on a cold December day. Even with the bleakness of winter and a thin coating of snow on the ground, the house and property were impressive.

Lynn told Rosemary that she had been an experiencer of the paranormal since childhood, as were other members of her family. This is a pattern often seen in extreme hauntings. A place can be quite active, but little of it may register on human occupants unless they have the right antenna, so to speak. An open and sensitive person can literally act as both a magnet and a catalyst. Put the right person in the wrong place and a paranormal maelstrom ensues. However, it is impossible to predict whether or not a sensitive person will *always* stir up phenomena. Every situation seems to depend on a peculiar mix of the energy of place, the presence of a portal, and the psychic attunement of the people. Even individuals who have little or no paranormal history can find themselves in paranormal pandemonium if conditions are right.

The patterns seen in extreme hauntings also occur in extraterrestrial abductions. Rosemary wondered if Lynn might be an abductee, given the descriptions of the bedroom visitations: the bed shaking, the ripped sheet, the reversed nightclothes, and the "man" trying to insert something into her mouth. However, Lynn had no pattern of activity that indicated ET interference. The activity seemed to be centered around the house as well as in it, and it better fit the profiles Rosemary had compiled over the years of residences in portal areas. Yes, there were ghosts on the property—but there were a lot more presences as well, and the evidence pointed to nonhuman ones.

For the investigation, Rosemary brought her Minibox ghost box, and did a real-time EVP session. There were numerous clear communications, including a male voice that said, *"Devil... do you have faith."* When asked, "Who are you?" a voice said, *"Dead."*

"Why are you here?"

"Waiting for something to go wrong," came the answer.

At the end of the session, they asked for any final messages. A voice rang out, *"Luuuucy... Luuuuucy... she can go now."*

The answer seemed to refer to Lucy the dog, but no one had any idea what that meant. Several months later, Lucy was diagnosed with an aggressive form of cancer. Was this message a threat or a prediction? Lucy showed signs of being as distressed as her owners. Did the stress damage her health?

On the second investigation visit, the Minibox was set up in the master bedroom for a session. A few minutes after turning it on, melodic chimes sounded in the room. Everyone, including Lynn and her son, heard them. There was nothing in the room that could make the sound of chimes, and it had not been part of a radio broadcast fragment.

Chimes, bells, music boxes and other mechanical melodic sounds are often heard in haunted places. The sounds simply manifest out of the thin air.

Over the following months, Rosemary made repeated visits to the house on Mayhem Road, and collected more EVP evidence on the Minibox. She had numerous conversations with Lynn, and kept a diary of activity.

Rosemary felt that Djinn were present in the mix, but not religious-type demons. She called John and asked him to come in on the case. On his first visit to the property, he agreed that nothing seemed to be demonic, and the excessive activity pointed to a combination of human ghosts, Djinn, shape-shifters, and entities and energy forms of unknown origin. "They're all having a field day," John said.

John and Rosemary were not optimistic about a permanent clearing, but felt that the activity might be lessened, provided Lynn and

Jim could get an upper hand. The "house on Mayhem Road" followed a pattern of other haunted homes that they had investigated in the past. In a showdown of persistent phenomena versus human beings, the phenomena often win, and the people depart for a calmer place to live. Even tearing a house down in a portal hot zone does not make a difference: the portal exists independently of structures in our dimension.

Rosemary made arrangements to conduct an overnight investigation at a new moon in order to witness and document more phenomena. Those plans were not to be. A few days prior to the investigation, Lynn's mother suffered severe injuries in a fall, and had to be convalesced at their home. The overnight investigation was off for an indefinite period of time.

Unfortunate accidents that delay or prevent investigation also are a common phenomenon in badly afflicted places. It was not the first time John and Rosemary have had "something" interfere in probes.

Meanwhile, unpleasant phenomena reigned at the house on a daily basis. Every now and then, markedly strange incidents stood out. Lynn and Jim were caught up in a wider web of the high strangeness that permeated a region extending well beyond their own property.

The mystery woman at the deli

One day Lynn stopped at a local deli. An older woman stood behind the counter with other employees; Lynn had the impression that she worked there. Lynn had never seen the woman before, but the woman seemed to know who she was. She commented to Lynn that she knew where she lived. In fact, she said, she knew a lot of what went on in the area—creepy things.

"You're very brave to live in that house," she said to Lynn. "I know what happens there."

Lynn was upset that a stranger seemed to know not only who she was, but where she lived, and what went on there. It felt like an invasion of privacy.

When Lynn relayed the incident to Rosemary, she said she wanted to meet the woman and interview her. Lynn returned to the deli to make arrangements. The woman was not there, and Lynn asked when she would return.

She was greeted with puzzlement from the other employees. No such woman had ever worked at the deli, and no one knew who she was.

Rice, rice everywhere

Another regular occurrence at the house was the mysterious appearance of loose, uncooked white rice. Piles of it, scoops of it, were found unexpectedly and in strange locations, as though a Rice Poltergeist was on the loose. Lynn liked to keep a small burlap bag of rice in the kitchen for cooking—but rice showed up everywhere but on a dinner plate. She would walk into the kitchen and find small piles of it on the counter or table, as though someone had dipped into the bag—which was always securely closed—and taken out a quantity. She would open the linen closet and find loose rice sprinkled all over the towels and sheets. Once Jim went to his athletic club to work out, and when he opened up his gym bag he found it full of rice.

Loose rice certainly gets one's attention, and it is most annoying to clean up. Was something getting a good laugh at their irritation? Lynn stopped keeping rice in the house, which diminished the rice events, but did not put a complete stop to them.

Why rice? Everyone puzzled over that one. Rice is a symbol of fertility and prosperity. It also is used to ward off and repel evil spirits. If nasty tricksters were responsible for the rice, then they were choosing the very substance that should keep them at bay.

Or, was something else intervening, such as a benevolent spirit working on behalf of Lynn and Jim? No clear answer emerged. The Rice Poltergeist fell into a category of typical Djinn tricks that seem to have no purpose, no rationale, and no resolution, and we chalked it all up to that.

Rice even showed up off site. Prior to moving into the house, Lynn had operated an import shop of home décor items in another county. She had closed the shop, and whatever remained unsold went into a locked self-storage unit. The items were boxed and sealed with packing tape. When a friend of Lynn's decided to have a summer tag sale, Lynn thought it was time to get everything out of storage and add it to the sale.

The storage facility was in another town some distance away from their home on Mayhem Road. One day, she and Jim drove to the facility and went through many of the boxes. They were still sealed with the original packing tape, and they had remained untouched in the unit, locked, for about two years.

Lynn opened up one of the boxes—and found inside a large quantity of loose white rice. The Rice Poltergeist had struck again!

A mystery trooper

Lynn and Jim did not take everything out of the storage facility on that day. The next day, Lynn went back to the storage unit by herself to retrieve the remaining items. When she got there, she discovered that, for some reason, the key would not work in the lock. It had worked the previous day with no problem. Try as she might, she could not get it to turn and open the lock. She even tried the units on either side, just in case she had made some weird mistake. Nothing.

Frustrated, she returned to her car to go home. What an irritation! It was the latest in a very long string of perplexing, unexplained and wearisome events.

Lynn's travel route took her north on an interstate known for several speed traps in both north and south directions. Lynn was careful not to speed anywhere she drove, but on this highway, she was always extra vigilant, keeping her SUV at sixty-five miles per hour or slightly below.

It was about 3 PM and traffic was light. Near one of the exits known to be a speed trap, Lynn passed what appeared to be an unmarked state trooper car pulled way off on the median, partly obscured by grass. It was pointing south in the opposite direction of oncoming traffic. There was something odd about it—it gave her the impression of a panther waiting to pounce.

Up ahead of her was a delivery truck pulled onto the right shoulder with its hazard lights flashing. Lynn moved from the slow lane to the middle lane, checking her speed. The next thing she knew, the unmarked "trooper" car was right behind her. She could see police lights in the grill, but the driver did not turn them on. Instead, he pulled into the fast lane as though he intended to pass her.

But the "trooper" car pulled straight alongside Lynn and paced her. She looked over at the driver, and he motioned her to pull off the highway. She complied. Oddly, the car pulled off in front of her, not behind her.

A tall, large black man wearing sunglasses got out of the vehicle and came up to her driver's side. Lynn already had her window down and her identification and registration in hand. The man was wearing a dark, short-sleeved uniform of some sort, but it was not obviously a trooper or police uniform. He wore no badge or American flag pin. No trooper hat. No radio. His shirt bore just a thin little name tag with a first initial and a last name. (Later, Lynn could not remember if he wore a gun.)

There followed a bizarre conversation in which Lynn felt like a mouse in a game of Alice in Wonderland cat and mouse.

The man took her license and registration, but looked mostly at Lynn. "Do you know why you were pulled over?" he said.

"No," said Lynn. "I wasn't speeding. I looked when I passed the truck. I was doing sixty-three miles an hour. I don't know why I was pulled over."

"What would you say if I told you that you *were* speeding?"

Lynn decided not to argue. "I guess you would know if I was," she said.

"I like that answer!" the man said enthusiastically. "I would know! I like that answer! I would know! I would know!" He went on for several minutes about what a good answer that was to his question. Lynn felt increasingly uneasy. *What is going on here?* she thought. *Who is this guy?*

Still holding her license and registration, he said, "Where do you live?"

She gave him the name of her town.

He repeated it uncertainly. "Where is that?" he asked, as though he had never heard of the place. She told him, thinking privately that this question was quite odd. A trooper in this area should know all the towns, especially the major ones.

"Where are you coming from?" he asked.

Lynn's unease increased. Legally, he was not allowed to ask such a question unless she was under suspicion of a crime. She decided to try and sound like nothing was wrong—they were just having a casual conversation. She told him where she had come from, and that she was on her way home.

"What were you doing there?" he asked.

Lynn gave him a long answer about going to the storage center to retrieve things for a tag sale, being strangely locked out, and what a frustrating day she was having. All the while, he stared intensely at her behind his black sunglasses. She had the feeling that he was trying to memorize her face. She tried not to look or sound nervous.

Abruptly, he handed her back her documentation. He returned to his car and drove off. No ticket, no warning, no explanation, not another word.

Lynn was shaken by the incident. When she arrived home, she had another surprise. One of the men she had hired to work around the house came up to her immediately. He was in a state of agitation. He told her about a strange incident in which he and his coworker, driving in his pickup truck, had been pulled over northbound on the same interstate by an unmarked trooper car. It was about the same time that Lynn was having her incident at another spot on the same highway. The "trooper" made him pull completely off onto an exit and stop. Like Lynn, the man was subjected to a weird conversation by the "trooper" but was given no ticket or warning.

Even stranger, his companion mysteriously fell into a deep sleep and could not be roused. He was unconscious throughout the entire incident.

This was similar to experiences in which a person's spouse or partner sleeps as though comatose through a terrifying bedroom episode, such as experienced by Justin Spurrier in "The Thing in the Stone Egg" in this book. It also happens to ET abductees. The purpose may be in part to isolate the primary witness. Thus, there is no one else to corroborate the story.

An unanswered question hung over these two "mystery trooper" events. What was it that could act up at the house and also create disturbances for Lynn, as well as others associated with her, off-premises in distant locations? What wanted to monitor her and let her know about it? Was nowhere safe?

A Taoist exorcism

The activity on Mayhem Road followed another pattern seen in portal areas. The pattern goes in waves that roll up and down, intense periods followed by lulls, then a restart in low-level activity that rises to a high pitch, followed by a sudden break, usually when the occupants are strained to their limit. In a way, it seems to be a deliberate and intelligent form of torture aimed at wearing down the psychological and physical reserves of the targets.

Lynn's acupuncturist, "Doctor T," offered to bring a high-level Taoist master onsite to perform an exorcism and cleansing. Rosemary, of course, wanted to be on hand to witness it. The master lived in another state, and soon the opportunity presented itself for him to visit. Lynn called Rosemary and left a message with the date and time. She never got the message—it simply disappeared from the phone.

The master arrived wearing a fine yellow robe, carrying a long sword, a Tibetan singing bowl, and water. He walked the property and the house and made his assessment. He performed exorcisms, brandishing the sword and using the singing bowl, and uttering incantations and chants. He drank water which he held in his mouth to infuse it with *chi*, and then sprayed it out at his targets. He went into the basement, refusing to allow anyone to accompany him. While he worked below, unearthly sounds issued forth: whining, moaning, and screaming. The master stayed overnight to continue his work.

When he was done, he informed Lynn that he had banished about fifteen entities. However, there was one—an old man—who could not be budged from the property. It was the same old man Lynn had seen herself.

The master informed Lynn that even though he had sent the others away, the land itself was "open" and they would return. "Your place will be quiet for a while," he said, "But they will come back."

This fit Rosemary's assessment of the property as resting on an active point in the local portal. The gateway could be quieted temporarily, but not closed permanently.

For a while, the house was calm. Then activity started to pick up again. Things were creeping back in. The peace ended.

Enough is enough

By the end of the summer, about nine months after Rosemary and John entered the case, Lynn and Jim decided to put their house up for sale. They were not being hounded out, she emphasized. The continual upsets were an ongoing drain, however, and the couple was tired of being subjected to the petty and unsettling pranks of the invisibles.

Rosemary could see a marked transformation in Lynn. She had been frightened and uncertain, and now she was clearly more in charge. She was determined to leave on her own terms. She told Rosemary that all the help had provided her realistic information on what was probably going on, as well as a realistic assessment of what could and could not be accomplished to lessen the activity.

There were other issues involved in the decision to move. Lynn's mother was spending more time at her Brooklyn apartment, but still required care at the couple's home. It was a long drive taking her mother back and forth every week, and Lynn wished to live closer to her mother's apartment to make the travel easier for everyone.

Lynn and Jim listed the house and then held their breath. Would "they" stay quiet in order to allow them to sell the place and move on?

The answer was soon forthcoming. A real estate agent brought over a family who seemed very interested in the property. Right before they arrived, a huge water stain spread over the ceiling of one of the bedrooms upstairs. The roof had never leaked there. Flustered, Lynn and Jim made excuses for the recent rain and promised it would be fixed. As soon as the prospective buyers left, the "water stain" disappeared.

Other things in the house malfunctioned, again without explanation. The deal fell through.

Black helicopters and Men in Black

About one month after putting the house on the market, and about three months after the mystery trooper incident, Lynn had another high strangeness event on the highway. Once again, she was traveling north on the interstate at about 3 PM. Traffic was light, and she was doing her usual speed at just below or at the speed limit. She was even more careful about speed since the incident with the strange "trooper." She passed the spot where the "trooper" had pulled her over. Her attention was momentarily diverted by three large black helicopters in a triangular formation that suddenly appeared right above her. One instant they were not there, the next instant they were. They appeared to be lifting straight up and higher into the sky, not flying off. Puzzled, she divided her attention between the road and the helicopters.

Suddenly right behind her, practically on her bumper, was a shiny black town car with dark tinted windows, flashing a small blue light on the driver's side of its hood. It looked more like an official limo, but could have passed for an unmarked trooper car. The light was one of those small magnetic clamp-on lights such as used on emergency vehicles when needed. It looked ridiculous and out of place on the town car.

Now what? Lynn thought. She pulled off to the shoulder and stopped her SUV. The black car pulled up behind her. She could not see the occupants because of the tint on their windows. Turning to look over her shoulder, she saw a man in a black suit get out of the *passenger* side of the car and walk up to her driver's side window. He was tall and thin with short black hair and beetle-like black sunglasses that completely masked his eyes. He wore a white shirt and a dark tie. His skin was pale white.

He peered at Lynn as she put her window down. She could feel an intense gaze despite the impenetrable cover of the sunglasses. "Show me... some identification," he commanded in a halting manner. His voice was odd and tinny, almost mechanical.

Lynn's heart thumped. This was another bizarre encounter that did not feel right. Silently, she pulled her driver's license out of her purse and handed it to the man.

He held it at arm's length and glanced at it, but redirected his gaze to stare heavily at Lynn's face. Again, she could feel his eyes boring into her even though she could not see them. It gave her a creepy feeling. It reminded her of the "trooper" who seemed to be trying to memorize her face. Her heart thudded away.

After a few minutes, he handed her back her license. Without a word, he turned, went back to the black car and got in on the passenger side. The car pulled out and drove down the highway, disappearing into the distance. She never did get a glimpse of the driver.

It was another strange encounter with no purpose—and no explanation.

Men in Black (MIB), as well as black helicopters, are prevalent in UFO cases, where contactees or witnesses are harassed by either or both. The MIB are usually described as Lynn saw the one: tall, thin, extremely pale skin, dressed in black, black sunglasses that obscure the eyes, or large, slanted black eyes. They drive black cars. They speak in an irregular fashion and sometimes do not make grammatical or logical sense. Sometimes they warn experiencers not to talk. Or, they act erratically and exude malevolence. In either case, the victims are left feeling frightened and vulnerable. Sometimes an encounter with an MIB is followed by poltergeist activity at home, feelings of being watched, and other high strangeness.

MIB also pop up in non-UFO circumstances. They are associated with black-eyed beings (in both children and adult forms), phantom monks, shadow people, and other sinister forms. There are female versions of them as well. Black-eyed beings have similar humanoid appearances and behavior, and sometimes accost people, leaving in their wake physical ill feelings and an onset of high strangeness phenomena. Shadow people, as noted earlier, are solid black silhouette forms taken by Djinn, whose pestering has a similar detrimental effect. Shadow people may also account for the many sinister "phantom monk" forms seen in years and centuries past.

The "trooper" and the MIB experiencer by Lynn were part of a big picture of harassment, morphing into many guises, popping up unexpectedly and in odd places. Djinn are capable of this kind of behavior, but the Phenomenon—with a capital P—seems to have an even bigger reach, and a deeper mystery.

As Rosemary was writing up this case, the Mayhem Road phenomena reached out and tapped her on the shoulder. One evening she met Lynn over a meal at a famously haunted tavern in the area. They went over details of events at the Mayhem Road house. The next morning, Rosemary found a silk women's leopard print scarf wedged between her back door and screen door, as though deliberately left by someone—or something. There was no plausible explanation for how it got there—no random wind, no passersby in the back yard—but it did seem to be a Djinn-like calling card, evoking the panther association of the mystery trooper, the cat and mouse games, and the black mystery cat-like thing seen on the property.

Something else even more mysterious happened as well.

Late one afternoon, Rosemary left her home to drive to John's house, and stopped by a Best Buy to do a quick errand. She parked her SUV in an isolated spot in the parking lot, well away from other cars. She was in the store for about ten minutes, and when she came out, she saw a black SUV parked next to her on her driver's side. It was facing in the opposite direction of her SUV, so that the two driver's sides were next to each other. There was nothing unusual about that—except that a large quantity of uncooked white rice was piled behind the black SUV's front tire on the driver's side. Rosemary estimated that it was about one pound in measure.

Now, who drives to a Best Buy parking lot, chooses an isolated spot to park right next to the vehicle of a paranormal investigator—and piles white rice behind one tire of their own vehicle so that the investigator cannot fail to see it? In fact, who drives around with uncooked rice, anyway, piling it against cars in parking lots?

The Djinn!

Postscript

The House on Mayhem Road is just one of an unknown number of residences affected by the Hudson Valley portal. How many other people live in unrest because of paranormal activity inside their houses, on their land, and even inside their heads, suffering from mental mayhem as well as physical? One thing we know for certain: The Hudson Valley and other portals John and Rosemary have investigated are but the tip of an interdimensional iceberg.

Rosemary stayed with this case for several years, until at last Jim and Lynn left the property. Many more bizarre things happened before the final moving box went out of the house.

The case is an example of how sometimes haunted landscapes cannot be cleared to the satisfaction of people. Throughout our history, we have always had places like that on Earth, where misfortune befalls those who occupy them. They are "demon haunted," that is, plagued by energies, presences, spirits, and entities that are problematic. These places may have always been that way—and they may never change.

12

A Spirited Liquor Cabinet

Rosemary here to tell you about one of my own ongoing experiences with an afflicted vintage liquor cabinet, and how the haunting took an unexpected turn.

My husband, Joe, and I love to pick up furniture and decor in antique shops and estate sales. Our home is chock full of previously owned items large and small, and nothing has ever come with a spirit surprise—until an autumn day when I acquired a liquor cabinet.

I was browsing one afternoon in one of my favorite local antique and estate shops when my attention was riveted by a large, stately black lacquer cabinet of Asian design. It was in excellent condition, with images of scenes and maidens done in gilded paint and inlaid mother-of-pearl and ivory. The cabinet was footed, and looked like it had storage galore: a main section with front doors that opened from the center out; a pull-down door to a top compartment, and side compartments. The lacquer was in pristine condition.

I did not realize the cabinet was for liquor until I opened it, and saw that the top compartment was for barware and the main compartment had a pull-out drawer with holes for different sizes of bottles. The side compartments had racks and shelves for glasses.

Perfect! I thought. Joe and I like to entertain, and this would make a nice show piece in our fireplace room.

I inquired about the history of the piece, but the store attendant had no information, other than the cabinet had just arrived at the shop about two days earlier.

"I'll take it," I said, and made arrangements to have it delivered.

While we waited for the cabinet to arrive, I did some research online, and discovered similar cabinets in varying condition and over quite a price range. Ours was in much better shape than most of the ones I saw online. They dated to the mid-twentieth century.

After the cabinet was delivered and installed in the fireplace room, I cleaned it inside and out. I discovered that it was stamped HONG KONG on the back. I filled the insides with crystal stemware and glasses, and bottles of liquor.

All the doors on the cabinet closed and opened easily with brass pulls. The front compartments had pulls shaped like little vases. None of the doors stuck, failed to stay closed, or had an unevenness to them.

All seemed peaceful with the new cabinet—until the next day.

Joe and I are in the habit of having our morning coffee in the fireplace room, where we light a candle and wake up to the day. When I passed by the new liquor cabinet, I was astonished to see that the brass pulls on the main compartment were inside out and crossed one over the other in an X fashion. They were jammed together so tightly that I could not undo them. It was impossible to open the main compartment where all the bottles had been stored.

"Did you do this?" I asked Joe, pointing to the latches.

"No," said Joe. He looked at the crossed pulls. "What the heck happened?"

We examined the pulls carefully. They appeared to have been deliberately manipulated. There was no way the pulls could have flipped over inside out on their own in our opening and closing the doors, let alone jam tightly together.

Front of the liquor cabinet (Courtesy R.E. Guiley)

We tugged on them and could not budge them loose. I was afraid of damaging the cabinet, and gave up. I didn't know how we were going to get them undone. The cabinet was as good as locked.

"I think we have a spirit attached to this cabinet," I said. "It either doesn't want anyone to drink alcohol, or it wants to keep the alcohol to itself!"

It took a great deal of tugging to finally disengage the crossed pulls. I opened the compartment and saw that nothing was disturbed inside. I then experimented with closing the compartment door to see if there was any way that the pulls could have flipped into place like that on their own—even though I knew it was not possible. I tried to duplicate the crossed pulls myself, and could not do it without risking damage to the brass pulls or the cabinet. In order to duplicate the mysterious inside out X, I had to flip the pulls up to show the underside, and then try to twist them around to make the X. I could not get them twisted. How something unseen had managed to do this feat was beyond me.

Left, pulls in normal position were found crossed, right (Courtesy R.E. Guiley)

After that, I could not pass by the cabinet without looking at the pulls. We expected it to happen again, or at least something else to happen in the house. But all was quiet.

Our house sits on enchanted land. Faeries and other beings populate the woodsy part of our property, and every now and then something passes through the house, or hangs around for a while. We have drop-in spirit visitors, too, who are attracted to evenings of entertainment and seances.

We regularly see shadow forms in certain parts of the house— they are benign residual imprints—and Joe has seen a phantom cat. Occasionally we hear footsteps in parts of the house where no one is present.

When I have worked on "Dark Side" research, such as the Djinn, we get rashes of poltergeist activity and coin apports—the Djinn are fond of dropping beat-up dimes, pennies, and nickels to let us know they are around and know what we're doing.

Once we had some company for the weekend to work on a Djinn project. Chris Mancuso, a paranormal investigator and filmmaker, and his wife, Cathy, came for the weekend so that Chris could give me some coaching on audio recording. I was going to attempt to record a narration of my book, *The Djinn Connection*. On the Sunday morning, Chris and I were in my office upstairs, and Joe was in his office down the hall. Chris and I had my office door closed, but we could hear the bath water come on in the guest bathroom. It sounded hard and fast, a faucet on full blast. I figured that Cathy was running a bath or shower.

The water ran and ran for a long time. Joe noticed it, too. Peeking out from his office, he saw that the bathroom door was ajar, which was odd, if Cathy was using the shower. Joe went downstairs and saw, to his surprise, that Cathy was curled up on the sofa in the fireplace room reading a book.

"Are you running the water in the bathroom?" he asked.

Cathy replied no, that she had taken a shower much earlier.

Joe went back upstairs and into the bathroom, where he found the water on full force.

There was no explanation, other than the fact that I was working on Djinn material… and strange things happen when you focus on the Djinn.

Despite the pranks, the house has always had a calm, peaceful atmosphere. We felt it the day we looked at it while we were house-hunting, and all our guests and friends feel it as well. It has its activity, but not in a negative way. The first time John visited the house, he commented on its peaceful atmosphere.

Now we had something new in the environment—a cabinet with something capable of fooling with its doors.

Whatever the spirit was, it laid low after the first incident. After some time had passed, I wondered if the spirit had "spent" itself on the brass pull caper and had moved on. I could not get a bead on anything attached to the cabinet.

I wrote a short article about it for my newsletter, *Strange Dimensions*. And, of course, Joe and I regaled our guests with the story.

The next incident happened when John came over one evening to discuss this book. We sat in the fireplace room and I told him the story of the cabinet and how I thought it must have a spirit attached to it because of the activity. I demonstrated how the pulls had been rearranged, though I could not do the job as completely as our unknown resident. John commented again on how peaceful the house felt, which is unusual when an attached object is present. I agreed, and commented that it was a mystery.

John, Joe, and I went out to dinner. John drove his own car so that he could leave straight for home from the diner.

When Joe and I returned to the house, we found the liquor cabinet had been played with again. One of the front compartment doors was open, and one pull was skewed to the side. I felt like we were the butts of a big joke. Ha ha! At least the trickster hadn't locked us out.

A few nights later, Joe and I were in the living room watching television. The living room opens to the fireplace room via French doors, and from the sofa in the living room, one can see an edge of the liquor cabinet.

Suddenly a movement caught my eye and I focused on the fireplace room. I caught a glimpse of a being, slightly taller than the liquor cabinet, standing in front of it. It was rust brown in color and looked like a silhouette. The head was smooth, like a cut-out, and there were no features for a face, though I had the impression that the being was looking at me. I could only make out the upper torso before it vanished, as though it disappeared into the cabinet.

"I just saw the spirit that must be attached to the liquor cabinet!" I exclaimed. When I described the being, Joe said he had had glimpses of something similar in the same area.

But if a spirit or being was attached to the cabinet, why had I not picked up on it when I looked at the cabinet in the shop? Something this strong and active should have stood out like a red flag. The mystery intensified.

Not long after that, Samurai Studios came to the house to do some shooting for a pilot for a television series on evidence of the afterlife. The pilot featured best-selling author Josie Varga interviewing experiencers and experts. My role concerned the phenomenon of dream visits from the dead.

Present were the owners of Samurai Studios, David and Holly Whitstock Seeger, and their son, and Josie's husband, John. After the filming, we all enjoyed a light buffet of food and social conversation. Comments were made on the cabinet, and so I told the story of the crossed pulls, and demonstrated how it could not be duplicated by mere human effort. I described the being I had seen. One of the party expressed an interest in a single malt scotch in the cabinet, so I got it and some crystal tumblers out and a few of us had toasts. The energy in the house was buzzing with all the activity and excitement about the pilot.

Everyone departed at the same time. I saw them out. As soon as I closed the door, I went to the liquor cabinet to put away the bottle of scotch. It was literally seconds since everyone had gone out. The front pulls on the cabinet were not hanging straight, but were inside out and skewed markedly to the right at an odd angle, as though they had frozen in mid-swing.

I was vexed. We had all been around the cabinet for hours, yet the spirit had waited until everyone was gone to mess around with the pulls. It had to have happened in a flash, sometime between ushering the guests out and turning around. Amazing!

I called John to discuss the ongoing activity, and the sightings of the rust brown being.

"I don't think it's attached to the cabinet," said John. "It must be something else. Your house feels pretty clear to me."

I had to agree. Joe and I had become accustomed to the low-level ongoing activity, but if something had arrived with the cabinet, it ought to be acting out in more ways. There was no escalation in other activity or any sense of unpleasantness, just periodic playing with the doors in a trickster-like fashion.

Then one morning, as I abruptly spilled some rice crackers on the floor, I realized that our cabinet trickster was our house faery. Since moving in, we had been aware of a little being that liked to hang about the house. Joe and I both sensed it more than saw it. It liked the kitchen, fireplace room, and living room, and rarely ventured upstairs.

In faery lore, food that hits the floor belongs to them. If we drop something, we put it on a saucer and leave it out for a while so the faeries can take the essence of the food. Our resident faery has a fondness for the rice crackers we eat, and it seems we are always "accidentally" dropping a few on the floor.

What if the house faery had taken a shine to the cabinet and figured out how to play with the door pulls, almost like a child with a toy? The energy of our reactions encouraged it to do more tricks, and perhaps even gave it enough energy to manifest for me to see it visually. To both of us, it all made sense.

Soon we were not the only ones to see the little figure.

One weekend our friend Judika Illes, an author and editor, came to visit, and we threw a dinner party for her. Judika helped put out the appetizers, including rice crackers. As she opened the box, she pitched forward as though shoved from behind, and the box went flying, with crackers spewing out all over the floor.

"I'm so sorry!" she apologized. "I don't know what happened— the box just flew out of my hands!"

I laughed. "Don't worry—it's the house faery. I guess he wants some crackers." I gathered up the pile on the floor and put them onto a saucer. "That should keep him busy for a while," I said.

That night, Judika was visited in her bedroom by a small, rust brown being with a smooth head and no facial features. She awakened in the middle of the night and sensed a presence standing in the corner of the room by the head of the bed. In the dim light, she was able to briefly see the figure before it melted into the wall.

"I had the impression it was just observing me out of curiosity," she told us the next morning.

We named the little being Brownie, in part because of its rust brown color, and also because brownies are a type of faery that like to reside in houses. They are supposed to be helpful beings, though they will cause upsets from time to time to get attention. We feel the presence is benign, and we continue to put out crackers and other tidbits for it to enjoy. We don't mind Brownie fiddling with the cabinet pulls, as long as he doesn't lock us out!

Our experiences with the liquor cabinet raised an interesting perspective on haunted objects. How many objects are not necessarily attached, but somehow energize dormant or low-level resident energy and presences into action? If the suspect object is removed, the energy source goes along with it, but not necessarily the spirit or being, which may then sink back into dormancy.

This explanation may not fit the more extreme, negative cases, in which an attached spirit acts out in marked and violent ways once it is in a new environment. It may fit less extreme cases, such as objects that go walkabout, discussed next.

13

The Mystery of Walkabout Objects

Two brothers operated a salvage business out of a self-storage facility where a large unit served as their workplace. Ralph and Leo stored their work benches and tools there, and every day they took apart machinery, tools, and other items for their valuable parts. Work turned quite weird after they landed a contract to take apart old cell phone towers. Suddenly something not human was intensely interested in what they were doing.

The brothers were unnerved by the daily appearance of a tall shadow man that glided in to stand by them and watch them work as they stripped components. The shadow man sometimes watched them work on computers, but it was the most interested in the pieces of cell phone towers.

The figure radiated malevolence and was unnerving. It would zip around and suddenly appear and disappear. Ralph and Leo also noticed tools missing. They would come to work in the early morning to find tools that they used on the cell phone tower components had gone missing during the night, or were misplaced. If missing, the tools usually resurfaced within a few days, but in a different spot in the workplace.

The case came to the attention of Rosemary, who attempted to investigate the activity with medium Karl Petry. They were able to conduct interviews with the two men, but were thwarted in several attempts to do nighttime surveillance with cameras and equipment.

The facility was locked at night, but Karl and Rosemary were given the access code to enter onto a keypad in order to gain entrance. With several other investigators, they made three attempts on three nights to enter the building, all of which failed. The codes never worked. Nor did a key that also was provided. Obviously, whatever presence was there did not want them snooping around and investigating.

Rosemary believed the shadow person was a Djinn using one of their favorite forms, a dark silhouetted male humanoid. The Djinn are affected by electromagnetism and electricity, and have exhibited a great deal of interest in human computer and telecommunications pieces.

The haunting and movements of tools went on daily. It was not feasible to relocate their workplace out of the storage facility, or to remove tools or cell phone tower parts.

After months of nearly daily appearances by the shadow man, one of the brothers tried remedial action. He brought a crucifix and a portrait of the Virgin Mary, and hung them on the wall over his workbench. Every morning, he said prayers for protection. Soon the shadow man stopped coming.

Did this tactic discourage the shadow man—or did the entity get what it needed and depart on its own?

There are three possible explanations for this shadow person haunting:

1—The shadow person was already haunting the storage facility and its attention was drawn to the cell phone tower parts.

2—The shadow person was attached to some of the parts and started acting out with the tools when the towers were dismantled.

3—The shadow person was not attached to either the parts or the environment, but was attracted for some purpose of its own.

The most likely explanation is the third, which Rosemary based on her extensive research of shadow people activity and Djinn.

It is easy to blame spirits for the unaccounted disappearances and reappearances of objects—but spirits (and entities) are only the tip of the iceberg. The case above, and those that follow, demonstrate the complications that often face investigators in trying to determine exactly what is going on, and why.

Now you see it, now you don't

The disappearance and movement of objects are one of the most common phenomena of hauntings. It is often blamed on human "ghosts," but more likely, intelligent, energized beings or spirits are doing the dirty work. In folklore, the faeries are famous for pinching objects and either relocating them to strange places, or making off with them altogether. Demons, Djinn, poltergeists, and unknown beings and spirits will do the same. Object thieves can be in place in a home and be dormant, then spring to life when something new comes into the household, or when new people move in. They can also be attached to objects that are brought into an environment.

John and Rosemary have examined scores and scores of cases of moving and disappearing/reappearing objects related to hauntings, spirit attachments, and other kinds of haunting activity. Investigators may be tempted to explain all such cases as spirit-caused, but there are far more complexities to consider.

Energized by a book

Rosemary received a report from a woman who was experiencing missing objects and other phenomena every time she tried to read one of Rosemary's books. Was something attached to the book? The woman was at her wit's end.

"I recently bought your book *The Djinn Connection*, but I'm having trouble reading it," wrote Chandra. "Whenever I do, things happen—tools disappear, electronics stop working or work weirdly, things that were right in front of me disappear! Can you give me any advice on how I can make this stop? In the distant past, I did have a very unsettling experience with a shadow person. Thanks in advance for any thoughts or suggestions. I would like to finish reading the book!"

Rosemary responded with some suggestions, and noted that it would take determining what was present, and why, to arrive at the most effective solution. One tactic she suggested was the "angry dismissal," in which a person uses a great deal of force to order an unwanted presence to stop its activity or depart.

Chandra had immediate success with the angry dismissal, and some of the missing objects reappeared.

Rosemary replied that the relief might be temporary. "You might have some resident spirit that has gotten energy from your attention to the Djinn book," she said. "As I mentioned, the why here and now are crucial bits of information."

Chandra acknowledged feeling "creepy" while she read the book—an emotion that a resident spirit might be able to take advantage of. Chandra said, "As I read your book, I was fascinated but began feeling creepier and creepier and I wondered, how did she ever write this???"

Certainly the reading of a scary book will not automatically draw in pesky spirits. There had to be more going on. Chandra then acknowledged that she experienced missing items on a consistent basis. The activity had kicked up because of her reading of the Djinn book.

"Occasionally, I encounter bouts of missing stuff, such as the hall table where I place my keys *without fail* are suddenly gone," she said. "Annoying little stuff, thankfully, nothing major. When I reach my max fed-up level, I actually stomp my foot and angrily shout '...put them back!' Then it stops for a while. I've always referred to them as 'gremlins.' Perhaps it's all the same?"

She went on, "I am a jeweler and I work out of my home studio. I have a lovely neutral-colored Pashmina scarf that I use as a background for photographing my jewelry. It disappeared last week, then returned after my shout-out a few days ago. Then, in the middle of doing my taxes, my calculator disappeared....and it still hasn't returned!"

I asked Chandra how long she had been living in her home, and when the activity had started. The Djinn book was now revealed as only part of the mystery.

"I've only lived in this place for the last two years, and this has been going on for most of my adult life," said Chandra. "It started with a shadow man choking me in a dream, and after managing to wake myself up, I found him still choking me in my bed! I thought—and hoped—that I wasn't fully awake. When I roused myself some more, he was gone. I still remember the glowing red eyes in the featureless face!"

"That sounds like Djinn," Rosemary answered. "It's possible you have a natural, extra sensitivity to the spirit realm. People who do, have a variety of experiences where ever they go. Since this started in adulthood, is there anything that changed in your life that coincided with the onset? Trauma, major change, or beginning of paranormal activity/study?"

"Yes, actually." Chandra said. "The shadow man thing happened just before I separated from my first husband, who was driving me insane. He was very emotionally abusive. In fact, at the time, I thought it was him acting out in my dream! Then, suddenly, I developed appendicitis, was taken to the hospital by ambulance and had surgery that night. The next morning, the surgeon came around and said, 'I don't know what was bothering you, but your appendix was fine—healthy and pink.' When I was released from the hospital, I went home and packed and left. So... trauma, major change and paranormal activity all rolled together! Would such a situation tend to predispose one to paranormal activity, or sensitivity to it?"

Rosemary replied that those circumstances could influence the onset of, or increase in, paranormal activity. "A lot of that fits patterns I have seen, especially with shadow people. They are magnetized by trauma, emotional upset, depression, and anger. They are vampiric in nature and feed off that. They also generate fear on top of it to magnify the energy. Your 'dream' and appendicitis scare fit that pattern. Not everyone who goes through upheavals is attacked by shadow people, but individuals who have a greater than normal sensitivity to the unseen make better targets. You might be one of those persons. Usually when people get their lives back in balance, however, the attacks abate, unless there is something else going on, which I suspect there is in your case."

Chandra then acknowledged that she had once undergone a past-life regression that revealed "a startling, and unpleasant possible explanation" for something going on in her life at the time. She did not provide details.

Sometimes issues with entities and spirits start in a previous incarnation and carry forward to another lifetime. Spirits, as well as the Djinn, have the capability of tracking people through time. They may not be active all the time, depending on circumstances. It is likely that Chandra's connection to the spirit world has a long time line, and reading Rosemary's Djinn book was only the latest caper.

This case is a good example of how there are often no quick and easy solutions to spirit interference, and investigators have to consider many possibilities. There is always more going on than meets the eye.

Jotts

Parapsychologists have addressed the unexplained disappearance and reappearance of objects from other perspectives, including space-time displacements that happen for unknown reasons, and the projection of intense human emotion. A term has even been coined to describe such events: Jotts, which stands for "just one of those things." Almost everyone gets "jottled" at some point, but some individuals experience the phenomenon more frequently than others, especially if they are participants in hauntings.

"Jotts" describes odd paranormal phenomena which do not fit into any prevailing paradigm. The acronym was coined by Mary Rose Barrington, a psychical researcher, former barrister, former president of the Oxford University Society for Psychical Research, and, since 1995, vice president of the Society for Psychical Research (SPR) in London.

Barrington has collected, classified, and catalogued numerous cases of jotts. Rosemary learned about her jotts research while on one of her trips to England. She attended a lecture meeting of the SPR and had a chance to chat with Barrington over tea and biscuits. Rosemary felt jotts are an excellent categorization for certain phenomena beyond explanation, and they may account for some paranormal activity in some cases of haunted places and objects.

There are two main classes of jotts. The more frequent of the two is "jottles," which concern displacements of objects, including phenomena associated with teleportation, apports, and poltergeist activity. The second is "oddjotts," which concern miscellaneous happenings that have no explanation.

The jottles are, according to Barrington's classifications:

Walkabout. An article disappears from a known location and is found later in another and often bizarre location, without explanation for how it got there.

Comeback. An article disappears from a known location and later—sometimes minutes or perhaps even years— mysteriously reappears in the same location. It may be a special case of walkabout.

Flyaway. An article disappears from a known location and never reappears. Flyaways may be Stage 1 walkabouts with an exceptionally long time-frame.

Turn-up. An article known to an observer but from an unknown location is found in a place where it was previously known to be. Turn-ups may be Stage 2 of a walkabout.

Windfall. A turn-up in which an article is not known to the observer.

Trade-in. A flyaway followed by a windfall that is closely similar to the article flown away.

Things that go walkabout

The most common jotts are walkabouts, which usually happen to small objects. Chandra's experiences are good examples of walkabouts that are probably due to spirit interference. Here is another example of a resident spirit that seems to be haunting a home:

> Walkabouts and comebacks happen quite frequently at my boyfriend's sister's house. Sets of keys disappear only to be found weeks, even months later in odd places. Remote controls vanish into thin air. I was at the house on one of these occurrences. Three of us must have searched the entire house, every cushion to every chair was lifted, furniture was moved, and her boyfriend even got so upset (it was his remote) that he took a knife and cut the back of the couch open just in case it had gotten shoved way down into the couch. Eventually the search was abandoned.
>
> Later that evening, another friend was being told about the incident. He pointed to the floor next to the chair and said, "Is that the remote?" It was on the floor in plain view, nothing over it or even by it.
>
> Hats and ball caps are also prime targets. They disappear from their shelf in plain view only to turn up in

unused closets or other rooms, sometimes even back on the hook. No one claims to have put them there. At this particular house, a jott occurs at least once or twice a week, maybe even more than they realize.

Some cases, however, have no known agents or causes. Consider the following two cases. The first was reported by a man:

Years ago I lived in a small trailer near the motel I worked for. One night I had to fetch something from the store. I checked for my wallet before leaving and found it missing. I searched the small trailer for nearly an hour, even checking the kitchen cupboards. By now I'm in near panic, and with good reason. My wages for the next two weeks were in that wallet and it vanished! I knew it was with me in the trailer, so searching outside seemed a bit too much; I did it anyway! I went back inside and started looking again. I searched the tiny living room then back to the kitchen. I returned to the living room, and on my return to the kitchen I saw my wallet standing out on the floor in front of the fridge. It truly took my breath away. There was no way I could have missed that wallet laying there; it was the first thing I set my eyes on when returning to the kitchen.

The next case was reported by a woman:

One time about eight years ago, I took my dog for a walk to the store. I live by myself, so I'm sure I put my house keys in my coat pocket. Upon returning, I couldn't find my keys! Fortunately, I had a spare one stashed outside, so I was able to let myself in. I tore the apartment apart, looking for the keys. I couldn't find them. I even retraced my steps to the store, looking at the ground every step of the way and went back into the stores, but nobody had them. Then a couple of days later, the keys reappeared on top of the coffee table. Most certainly, that was a place I had looked before.

Another time, I had a piece of azurite that I used in my meditations. I was unable to find it for a time, then one time when I was returning home, it was on the ground just in front of the door. I can't remember for how long it was gone, but it was more than a few days.

And another example:

For the past few years, things—eye glasses, keys, books—have disappeared at my house and shown up in bizarre locations. For example, when I take my glasses off, I usually put them down by computer, but once when I went back to retrieve them, they were gone. I found them days later on top of the refrigerator. I used to chalk these disappearances to the antics of my fourteen-year old son, but I'm not so sure any more. Besides, he swears up and down to have never touched some of these items.

Flyaways

Most unsettling are the flyaways, objects that go missing and are never seen again, such as Jim's wedding ring in "Hudson Valley Havoc." The following case has unusual characteristics:

I took some jewelry to a Spiritualist Church in New York to be "read." I had a mysterious pair of cufflinks come down to me from my grandmother (previously seen over my shoulder in a spontaneous vision by an animal communicator). I had first attempted to practice the art of psychometry with one of these cufflinks, and after fifteen minutes got a very clear, startling image of Jesus in side view, but instead of praying hands he was gazing upward into a bright light.

Intrigued, I brought it to the psychic who held it in her hands for a moment. Then her eyes flew open and she exclaimed, "It's beating like a heart!" As I left the darkened room full of other mediums doing fund-raising readings, I could not find the other cufflink. Looking back, I now know the exact moment it disappeared during the reading, as I felt very uneasy and began to search for it. The cufflink was never found; the church members believe it was taken by Spirit.

However, with the help of a genealogist, I was able to trace the other one to the small state of San Marino in the Italian Alps—it is the seal of the founding hermit, but has no connection to my ancestry I know about! I use this one on a chain as a dowsing aid—it works great.

Did some spirit decide that at least one cufflink belonged back in San Marino—or elsewhere in the astral realm? We will never know.

Windfalls and trade-ins

Jotts such as windfalls and trade-ins are much less common than walkabouts and fly-aways. Here is an example of a windfall:

> Four or five years ago, I worked as a cashier at a gas station and tobacco shop out of Lewiston, Idaho, on the Nez Perce reservation. When it was time for my quick break, I went outside to sit down in the dark at a small table and put my hand into my sweater pocket to get a Kleenex. My hand touched something strange and I pulled out a key, with the number 18 on it. I was stunned—it looked like an old motel key! Nowadays they all use the card keys. I still have it, on my keychain. I'll never know how it got in my sweater pocket.

Were these people random victims of opportunistic spirits such as tricksters or low-level demons? Cases that do not have continuing phenomena, or other kinds of phenomena as well, are difficult to assess.

Sometimes jotts cases can be explained by absentmindedness and slips of memory—we think we left an object in a certain location, when in fact we placed it somewhere else. But when objects go missing and turn up in bizarre, unlikely locations, such as the stories above, a paranormal factor must be taken into consideration.

Attention-seeking from the dead

There are cases in which moved objects may be due to actions of the dead who are trying to get the attention of the living.

In the following example, a woman describes an unusual jott that may have been a signal from a deceased boyfriend:

> One evening I was pulling into a huge Wal-Mart parking lot and reaching for my travel cup (with lid on it) and I heard the silver flat knob on the radio button fall off and go "clink" somewhere in the car. I got upset because I thought I'd glued it back on well enough to stay! (I have an old car.) I took a quick drink of coffee and froze— there was something hard in my mouth! I took it out and there it was, the knob from the radio selector! Don't know how long I sat there thinking it simply wasn't possible, especially since my cup had the lid on, but there it was. I wandered around Wal-Mart, couldn't really remember what it was I needed, finally got a few things and went home. My psychic friend I called told me it was my deceased ex-boyfriend trying to get my attention—and I did hear his voice at a later time after he'd died. Well, it worked!

Jotts have no logical explanation, and leave experiencers scratching their heads. The explanation that fits best, and makes the most sense to a person, becomes the preferred interpretati

Are jotts teleported?

Teleportation is the disappearance of an object in one location and its reappearance in another. It's as though an object dissolves and then reassembles. Teleportation is a familiar device in science fiction; the transporter technology of *Star Trek* is probably the most famous example. But teleportation was considered impossible from the standpoint of quantum physics.

Scientists once did not take the subject seriously because it was believed to violate the Heisenberg uncertainty principal of quantum mechanics. Teleportation technically is the construction of an exact replica of the original object—atoms of the same kinds arranged in exactly the same pattern as the original. According to the Heisenberg uncertainty principal, the act of scanning, observing, or measuring an object disturbs it and prevents perfect replication. In 1993 scientists demonstrated that perfect teleportation is possible in principle, but only if the original is destroyed.

That view changed in 1997, when scientists in Austria and Denmark successfully teleported photons without destruction of the original. A big breakthrough occurred in 1998 when physicists at the California Institute of Technology announced the first quantum teleportation with a high degree of fidelity. The Cal Tech team teleported a "squeezed" light beam a distance of one meter. Then in June 2002, scientists in Australia successfully teleported a laser beam.

These advances have tremendous implications for new technologies in quantum computing and telecommunications—but no one yet knows how to apply teleportation to materials having mass. (Photons have no mass.) However, it is probably only a matter of time before "quantum leap" becomes a reality.

Christianity has teleportation explained, at least in certain cases. In religious literature, there are miracles of teleportation, called "miraculous transport," in which a saint instantly seems to travel from one distant location to another, or manifests an object. The miracles are credited to God's intervention in the world.

But how do spirits accomplish teleportation? No one has a good answer. Disappearing and reappearing objects abound in the paranormal—in hauntings, séances, spirit interference, and in cases of demonic possession. The displacement of objects happened frequently in the famous case that served as the basis for William Peter Blatty's best-selling book, *The Exorcist* (1971), made into a film in 1973. The victim, a boy, was successfully exorcized in 1949. Similarly, the Smurl Haunting, which afflicted a family in West Pittston, Pennsylvania, from 1985-1987, involved moved objects.

In our first book, *Haunted By The Things You Love*, we feature a number of haunted object cases where household objects went walkabout once a spirit was loose. Afflicted dolls and clown dolls in particular relocated themselves off shelves, chairs, and even from rooms. Some of the cases were attributed to spirits of the dead, and others to unknown spirits and demonic beings.

Rosemary's Djinn cases have instances of objects that vanish and are found in unlikely places. In one case, a man's car part went missing and wound up in a box of books 400 miles away in Rosemary's basement. Sometimes the stolen objects are returned, sometimes they are not.

Jot-prone people

Some people do not have to live in a haunted house to experience frequent jotts—they have them where ever they go. Do such individuals have spirits attached to them, or is there another explanation? Perhaps they carry an energy that affects physical space around them. In the next case, jotts run in a family:

> My daughters (teen and preteen) and I have jotts all the time. I think it runs in the family because I've seen my mother have them, too. I can name three specific incidences of jotts that occurred. When I lived at home, my mother and I were looking for the car keys everywhere because we were running late for an event (my older brother's graduation). Finally, my mother said, "All right, that's enough, give them back!" and the keys dropped on a table that was clear of everything else with an audible clank. We had looked there and nothing else was on the table before, and no one else was in the house or in that room at the time. My mother said, "Thank you," and out the door we went. She never explained it.
>
> The other time, or rather times, I liked to knit or crochet things to pass the time—no cable TV. I was still living at home and in my teens, and when I would put my yarn and needles down in the living room, they would always end up on my bed upstairs. Always, regardless of who was home at the time. My mother tested it once or twice and it happened to her. When she walked out of the room, they would somehow be upstairs. It used to freak my dad out and he wouldn't discuss it with her when she brought it up, saying he didn't want to know about that stuff.
>
> The third happened to my oldest daughter (fifteen) this year. She took her cell phone to a friend's

home when she spent the night. Later, it went missing and they tore the house apart and her friend's bedroom, and no phone. My daughter's friend's family searched for a week. We just figured my daughter just lost it somewhere else. When she went to her friend's home two weeks later, she entered her friend's bedroom and the cell phone was sitting on top of the previous day's laundry in plain view of the door. My daughter spotted it right away. It couldn't have survived a trip through the wash and work yet it was perfectly fine, and the laundry had been folded with the phone on top of the basket. Her friend and her family have no explanation for it.

Jotts happen to my family all the time, but these are ones that are the strangest. Usually I give up looking for whatever is lost and just ask aloud to have whatever took it give it back and I always say thank you just in case. I almost always get the item back in a place that has been thoroughly searched. I've noticed it seems to happen more now that my girls are getting into their teens, even when they are not home.

A century or so ago, people would have blamed such episodes on the faeries, demons, or even the dead, and it was a common practice to ask—or demand—for missing objects to be returned. Chandra, as you recall, angrily demanded for her missing objects to come back, and they did.

Apports and asports

Jotts are first cousins to apports and asports, which figure prominently in mediumistic activity. Apports are objects that appear out of the air, seeming to come from nowhere, and for which no explanation exists for how they arrived. The word "apport" comes from the French term *apporter*, meaning "to bring." The tem is also applied to walkabout jotts, objects that are suddenly in a place where they have not been before,

Psychical research literature defines an apport more narrowly as a small object that materializes in the presence of a medium or adept, as though it has been formed from thin air or has passed through solid matter. The materialization or teleportation is said to be done by the spirits who are present around the medium.

Mediumistic apports

Apports were a common phenomenon of Spiritualist séances, especially in the nineteenth and early twentieth centuries. Mediums said they combined their energy with that of the spirits present to produce flowers, perfumes and other objects. The phenomenon was studied by psychical researchers. Other apports have included vases, books, dishes of candy which moved about the seance table for the sampling of each sitter, and live birds, animals and sea life, including lions, hawks, buzzards, and lobsters. Some mediums were found to hide apports on their person before a séance and then produce them in the dark, while others produced apports with no normal explanation.

Agnes Guppy and Eusapia Palladino, both famous mediums in the nineteenth century, were renowned for their apports, which included flowers, fruit, sea sand, and ice. Palladino also produced disagreeable apports such as dead rats!

Guppy was herself an apport at a séance conducted by two of her protégés, mediums Frank Herne and Charles Williams, in 1871. One of the sitters at the séance jokingly asked if Guppy could be brought in. She was an enormously large woman, and the sitter thought this would be an impossible feat for the spirits to perform. According to reports, Guppy, who lived about two miles away, materialized in about three minutes. She was in her dressing gown, dazed, sitting in the center of the séance table and holding a pen and account book. She said that just as she was writing the word "onions" in her household ledge, she found herself whisked through the air at tremendous speed.

American medium Arthur Ford witnessed and heard stories of apports at seances and in times of crisis or need. One woman told him how silver dollars and gold pieces always appeared on her floor or in her hatbox whenever she had to have money for a needy person. In checking, she discovered the coins always bore the date of money the government had declared lost.

Ford reported the appearance of apports at one seance in England at the home of medium Catherine Barkel, which included Sir Arthur Conan Doyle and Ford among the sitters. After Barkel went into a trance, her Indian spirit guide and control took over and announced that the "little people" (faeries) had brought the sitters some valuable objects which had been lost on ships wrecked at sea or in other ways. Immediately precious stones, one for each of the sitters, appeared in Barkel's hand in her lap. Doyle took them to a jeweler, who appraised them at several hundred pounds. Ford's stone was a garnet; others were diamonds, amethysts, emeralds, and rubies. The sitters had them set in jewelry.

Perhaps the most unusual apports were produced by Charles Bailey, the pseudonym of an Australian medium who excited much interest on the part of psychical researchers. Born around1870, Bailey enjoyed a fifty-year career in mediumship until his death in 1947. He discovered his mediumistic powers at age eighteen. Early on, his controls announced he had a gift for apports and then produced the first one, a stone dripping with sea water, said to be conveyed from the ocean by a spirit. Among the many apports Bailey produced were live birds in nests with eggs; live fish, crab and turtles; a barely alive small shark; seedlings growing in pots of earth; an Arabic newspaper; rare coins and antiques (the value of which later were said to be grossly exaggerated); a human skull; a leopard skin; a huge piece of tapestry; precious stones; and clay tablets and cylinders said to bear ancient Babylonian inscriptions.

Bailey's method was to enclose himself in a double-sewn canvas bag with only his head and arms out, and seals placed at the neck and wrists. Efforts to test Bailey were thwarted by his spirit controls, who insisted on working in the dark.

He was searched prior to donning the bag, but was never undressed. Skeptics believed he hid apports on his person, or in hollow heels of his rather high-heeled boots (he was a very short man), and then pushed them out through an undetected hole in the sack. Once, he was caught with his boots off, and he also was exposed producing fake spirit materializations. Two exotic live birds he once produced as apports were taken to a local bird dealer for the purpose of identifying the species; the dealer recognized the birds as two he had recently sold to a man, and later identified Bailey as the purchaser. Bailey retorted that the dealer was a "stooge" of the Catholic Church.

Apports are still current seance phenomena. The famous Scole Experimental Group in England, which engaged in mediumship from

1994-98, produced some remarkable apports, including a pristine copy of the *Daily Mail* newspaper dated April 1, 1944. Skeptics might have thought that to be an April Fool's hoax, but an analysis showed that the paper and ink were of war-time origin, and the newspaper was printed on an obsolete letterpress. Numerous other small objects were apported. A photo of a token or coin with hieroglyphics was determined by the British Museum to be a modern imitation of an Ottoman coin used for weddings and in jewelry.

Several theories have been advanced by psychical researchers to explain apports:

- They are brought from other dimensions by spirits.
- They are drawn from other dimensions by the will power and magnetic pull of the medium.
- They are objects already existing on the earth plane which are forcibly disintegrated by the medium, transported, and reintegrated in another location.

According to medium John W. Bunker, a medium must put all his spiritual energy, or magnetic current, at the spirits' disposal in order to manifest apports.

Asports

Asports are like walkabout and flyaway jotts—objects that disappear and either reappear in an odd location, or vanish forever. During the height of physical mediumship in the late nineteenth century to early twentieth century, spirits of the dead who dropped in on séances would sometimes cause objects to disappear and reappear.

Eusapia Palladino was known for having spirits take the valuables of her sitters, much to their consternation. Sometimes the sitters would be relieved to find their goods relocated to their homes—but often they went permanently missing. Whether they were kept as treasure in the afterlife or some spirit realm, or secretly landed in the vaults of Palladino, was never known.

Poltergeists

Poltergeists are mischievous and sometimes malevolent spirits who disrupt an environment with a variety of rude disturbances. "Poltergeist" comes from the German words *poltern*, "to knock," and *geist*, "spirit." Poltergeist cases have been recorded from ancient Roman times to the present, and have been studied extensively by psychical researchers and parapsychologists since the 1890s.

In earlier times, poltergeist activity was attributed to faeries, demons, trickster-type spirits, the devil, and the restless dead. Early reports cite rock- and dirt-throwing, flying objects, loud noises, strange lights, apparitions, terrible smells, raps, physical and sexual assaults, and shrieks. Modern cases include all of those as well as interferences with technology, especially electrical items, computers, and phones.

Poltergeist activity usually starts and stops suddenly, often without apparent reason. It may last from a few hours to years, but rarely lasts longer than a few months. Activity rarely takes place when no one is at home, and usually occurs when a particular individual, or agent, is present.

A seminal study of worldwide poltergeist cases from 1800 to the present was done in the late 1970s by English researchers Alan Gauld and A.D. (Tony) Cornell. They identified sixty-four significant characteristics, the most common of which were movement of objects. Sixty-four percent of the 500 cases they examined featured movements of small objects, and 36 percent involved the movement of large objects such as furniture.

The rise of Spiritualism and physical mediumship brought a change in attitudes toward poltergeist effects. Fewer and fewer case were blamed on demonic forces and witchcraft, and more and more were attributed to the spirits of the dead demonstrating their presence to mediums and sitter at séances, such as the apports and asports mentioned earlier.

Even back then, evidence surfaced that more than spirits might be involved. Sir William Barrett, a nineteenth-century physicist and one of the founders of the Society for Psychical Research in London, witnessed poltergeist activity during visits to a home in Ireland where a widower and his five children lived. The activity centered on the twenty-year-old daughter, and Barrett wondered if she might somehow be the source or cause of the activity. Barrett also found that the poltergeist responded to his mental requests for knocks. In four successive trials, Barrett silently asked the entity to knock a certain number of times, and at each time it correctly complied. Who or what was really causing the activity?

In the early twentieth century, psychical researcher Nandor Fodor was one of the first to propose that at least some poltergeist cases were due to humans projecting an intense energy, not spirits. Fodor was roundly criticized for this view, but in later decades, more parapsychologists agreed with him.

A few decades after Fodor, Ian Stevenson, a psychiatrist and parapsychologist, said that spirits of the dead were too often overlooked as causes. Stevenson noted that living agent cases were characterized by meaningless raps; random movement of mostly light objects; short and simple trajectories; much breakage of objects; activities localized around a person, usually under the age of twenty; and relief of symptoms with psychotherapy. Cases attributed to the dead (as well as other spirits) were characterized by purposeful movement of larger and heavier objects; complicated and long trajectories; little, if any breakage; meaningful raps in answers to questions; phenomena sometimes localized around a person; and relief of symptoms with exorcism, placation, or intercession.

Gauld and Cornell found that only 2 percent of their cases were blamed on demons. Despite malevolent behavior, the spirits never identified themselves as "demons." Rather, that was an interpretation made by victims, who then called in clergy for exorcisms, thus reinforcing their belief. Demonic cases were more common in non-European/American cultures.

Since the Gauld-Cornell study, attitudes toward poltergeist cases have shifted again in the West, primarily due to the rise of ghost and demon hunting shows on television. Instances of disturbances, including moving and disappearing objects, are usually blamed on trickster or demonic spirits, or else angry spirits of the dead, by paranormal investigators. Few investigators consider the possibility of human-generated effects.

Like most things in the paranormal, many cases are not black-and-white, but blur with combinations of unexplained, human, and even hoaxed phenomena. The famous Enfield Poltergeist of England, which occurred from 1977-79, featured, among many effects, thrown, moving, and flying objects. The principal investigators were Maurice Grosse and Guy Lyon Playfair of the Society for Psychical Research. The case involved unknown and alleged spirit activity, child-centered psychokinesis, and hoaxing by the children, all of which muddied an analysis of exactly what was going on. The child who was the focal point was puberty-aged, a typical time for repressed emotions and emerging sexuality. The family had gone through a difficult divorce and relocation to a council house (subsidized housing for the poor). Complicating things even more was the fact that the two girls in the family had played with a Ouija board, and possibly had engaged a trickster spirit. Playfair opined that an "entity" was involved in the case but did not label it demonic.

Psychokinesis

Human-generated poltergeist effects are attributed to psychokinesis (PK), or the ability to move objects with the mind. PK has been put forward as one explanation that could account for some cases.

Emotional psychokinesis

A person's emotional state may be an important factor in jotts. The intensity of emotion may exert a force that somehow interacts with the properties of space and time—sort of an "emotional psychokinesis," an influence of mind over matter. Whether or not this would involve the participation of spirits or entities is not known.

Intense emotion and turmoil are cited in the following case of a comeback jott, an object that reappeared where it had last been seen:

> I have a laptop computer and use it to upload CDs to my iPod. The cable that connects the iPod to my computer is white and usually I keep it attached to the laptop. I had been sick over the weekend and took the white cable off because I had moved my laptop and didn't want to trip on a dangling cable. When I remove the cable, I always leave it in my family room, usually right near the sofa.

Yesterday, I wanted to do an upload and looked for the cable. It was nowhere in the family room, not near the sofa, not anywhere. I lifted pillows, pushed furniture, took every item on any surface and removed it, pored through drawers. Nothing in the room is white and the cable usually stands right out, but it was gone! When my husband came home, he went through everything in the room with no luck. We each searched the same area over and over.

Today, before I left the house, I went through the same search again with no luck. I figured I'd buy another on my way back home, which is what I did. I walked into my house, put down the package with the new cable, and went to the bathroom. When I walked out of the bathroom, I turned my head towards the sofa area and there was the cord, neatly coiled up on the dog crate right next to the sofa—just where it should be. But no one had been in the house.

My kids are grown and my husband was still at work. Both dogs were crated—not that either one of them could have coiled up the cord and placed it where it was. I didn't touch the cable because I wanted my husband to see it when he walked in. He was astounded!

Yesterday was a very tense day. I was running for office and yesterday was election day. I was more nervous and jumpy than you could imagine—not at all like myself. It was in that atmosphere that the cord disappeared. Today, as everything settled back to normal, there was the cord, practically speaking to me and saying, "Here I am, all tidy and waiting to be used!"

The emotions may have been sufficient for a one-off PK event, a temporary disappearance, or perhaps even a temporary time displacement.

Other states of conscious may affect the occurrence of jotts as well. People who spend frequent and long periods in creativity, healing, and meditation—all of which transport consciousness beyond linear time—may be more likely to have PK-type jott experiences.

RSPK

RSPK stands for "recurrent spontaneous psychokinesis," a hypothesis put forward in the latter twentieth century by parapsychologists William G. Roll and J.G. Pratt, who studied poltergeist cases. Roll hypothesized that there were patterns of recurrent PK, including the movement of objects, that were expressions of unconscious PK on the part of the individual who was the agent, or focal point, of the unusual activity.

Roll profiled the typical RSPK agent as a child or teenager who harbored repressed anger from some type of stressful situation in the household. PK was an unconscious way of expressing hostility without fear of punishment. The individual was often completely unaware of the psychic energy causing disturbances. Afterward, he or she experienced feelings of pleasure and happiness without knowing why.

Roll noted that the RSPK agents were often in a poor state of health, either mentally or physically, and thus were predisposed to stressful events. The phenomena could sometimes be ended by a relief of their distress, or by psychotherapy.

One of Roll's most famous RSPK cases was "The Miami Poltergeist," which he investigated in 1966 with Pratt. The Tropication Arts warehouse in Miami was experiencing unexplained movements of objects, such as toys and merchandise flying off the shelves seemingly on their own volition. The activity started in mid-December 1966. The RSPK agent was eventually identified as Julio Vasquez, a nineteen-year-old shipping clerk whose life was in turmoil. When Vasquez left his job on February 1, 1967, the activity abruptly halted. The researchers documented 224 unexplained incidents involving objects.

Space-time displacements

Yet another explanation for moving objects is space-time displacement. Somehow an object gets "lost" in time and perhaps space as well. It dematerializes and then rematerializes, sometimes where it was last seen and sometimes in another location. Is there some strange configuration of circumstances that makes this happen? Perhaps it is an effect that also allows for the participation of spirits, the dead, or the living—or all of them in any given case.

One of the strangest displacement cases in Rosemary's files concerns a woman's automobile that apparently went walkabout. The entire episode was permeated by a strange atmosphere, as though reality had shifted:

Years ago, when Christmas shopping for a present for my mother, I was going round and round the block, wanting to park on the other side of the street, but no empty space. Finally, I parked on the original side of the street I'd started out on, walked to the end of the street, and went in the end door of the building. I didn't find anything, and since it was almost 5:30, I thought I'd just come back another day. I trudged back through the slushy snow to the car—but the car wasn't there! I stood there dumbfounded. My footprints were still in the slush where I'd stopped and looked at a sign on a saw-horse, then turned and walked to the end of the building.

Immediately I thought someone had stolen it, so I looked up and down the street, but there was no traffic at all and an eerie silence—no birds, no traffic on the long bridge across the river behind me, nothing, just fog and silence. To make matters worse, all the stores up and down the streets were closed and no lights on. I didn't have a cell phone then, and couldn't call anyone to come help me or take me to a phone to report my stolen car.

Finally, I walked around the corner and looked down the other side of the street—and literally froze. There was a Monte Carlo just like mine, perfectly parked just where I originally wanted to be. It seemed like hours before I slowly walked up to it and slowly put my key in the lock and turned the key. The door opened and I got in and looked around and started crying, sure I was having a nervous breakdown. I was so upset I almost couldn't remember how to even get home.

When I did get home, I just stood and looked out at the car and wondered if my "intent" to park on that side of the street actually made it happen or what! Does anyone really believe me when I tell them what happened?

I don't think so. I have trouble myself believing it. So it
was either a "big apport" or simply a "time traveling car."

Coins

Finally, we must consider the peculiar mystery of coins. Spirits and
entities are fond of taking coins, and some of them—spirits as well as
Djinn, angels, and the dead—deliver them. Coins apports are especially
important for John Zaffis later on in this book.

Coins and tricksters

In lore, faeries—who are quite the tricksters when they want to be—
have a disdain for money and freely bestow it upon favored humans by
materializing coins and gold. They also will turn human coins to turnips,
coals, and stones when people displease them—a trade-in jott that no
person wants to get.

Trickster entities both take and leave coins. Men in Black and
Women in Black sometimes are fascinated by coins that people have.
They will ask for the coins or brazenly take them, and then vanish. Black-
eyed beings will do the same. The coins become flyaway jotts, never seen
again.

Conversely, the Djinn will leave coins as calling cards. Rosemary
has a jar full of coin apports related to Djinn cases. Pennies, nickels,
dimes, and occasionally quarters have appeared in odd places, at
appropriate timing, as though the Djinn want humans to know that they
are watching. She has even seen coins fall out of thin air.

The Djinn coins are roughed up as though they have been sanded.
Is this a phenomenon of interdimensional transport, or something the
Djinn do to distinguish their apports from ordinary coins?

Men in Black, Women in Black, black-eyed beings, and shadow
people may be just a few of the forms the Djinn take when harassing
humans. Perhaps they steal coins in one form and return them in other
forms, even invisible ones.

A dramatic Djinn coin manifestation occurred to Rosemary
during a filming event. She was taping for the premiere episode of
American Mysteries and Monsters in Pt. Pleasant, West Virginia, at the

end of a Mothman Festival. The stage was set for trickster phenomena: Pt. Pleasant was the capital of weirdness during the Mothman wave of 1966-67, and still sports a great deal of paranormal activity today. The filming took place in the Lowe Hotel, the only hotel in town and a building with a lot of haunting phenomena.

Rosemary was talking about haunted landscapes and the Djinn, and about the Djinn exerting their "land rights," when suddenly a klieg light in the back of the room exploded with tremendous force, startling everyone on the set. "That's the Djinn," Rosemary said. "They've just weighed in with their opinion."

Everyone took a break while the broken light cooled enough so that it could be replaced. One of the crew commented that klieg lights usually don't explode—if they are going out, they just lose their light. The crew left and went outside.

Joe, Rosemary's husband, was downstairs in the lobby. She called him up and told him what happened. They searched around the broken light and into a linen closet. There was nothing on the floor but shards of the light. Turning around, they spied a coin on the floor, up against the light pole, where nothing had been just a moment before. It was a dime, very abraded, as though roughly sanded.

The Djinn had left a calling card.

When filming resumed, Rosemary showed the dime, and explained that it was an apport. The exploding light was a dramatic example of phenomena that had been caught on camera.

None of the footage, including the exploding light, was aired. Everything concerning the Djinn wound up on the cutting room floor. No explanation was ever given.

Coins in paranormal investigations

Coin apports occur in many paranormal cases and investigations, where investigators suddenly see a coin where none was moments before.

Cheryl Alsippi, co-founder of the ALKO-PSI investigation group, documented a case in a home in Pennsylvania in which a penny appeared and then seemed altered in some way:

> Two investigators walked into one of the bedrooms that had been the location of reported spirit sightings and

upon initial scan of the room, a round object showed up on the thermal, lying on the bed. When they checked there, they found a penny. [One of the investigators] initially snapped a photo of it with the thermal camera. About two to three minutes later, the rest of us came in and I placed a recorder down beside it and started an EVP session. At that point, he snapped a second photo and the only thing that showed up this time on the thermal was the recorder. The penny had already "changed" and was no longer showing hot (or cold).

The appearance of the penny was an unexplained phenomenon of the haunting, as was the unexplained change in the penny itself.

Angel coins

Angels are known for leaving feathers as a sign of their presence, but they also leave coins. Gold-colored, quarter-size coins with an identical image of an angel on both sides are reported as mystery apports by people who say the coins appear in times of emotional distress and need. People who are grieving lost loved ones or who are down on their luck find fresh, shiny angel coins at their feet on the street, in drawers of furniture at home, on the floors of their homes, in purses and pockets, and even given in change when they make a purchase at a store. They take the coins as a "sign from heaven" that they are being comforted or their luck is about to change.

Rosemary has documented angel coin apports that go back for years. She has found that the coins are manufactured by industrial companies and used by religious charities in solicitation letters—but how would these coins show up out of thin air, as if by magic, to people who need spiritual comfort?

Pennies from heaven

Angel coins are not the only coins to manifest mysteriously in times of stress. Pennies are the most common coin that appears when people feel they need a lift or a boost of luck. Sometimes it is harder to assess the appearance of a penny on the ground or street, as people often lose small change. But if the appearance of a penny coincides with a state of mind or a meaningful event, it carries a powerful significance to the finder—and that is the important side of it.

John had a penny fall out of the air in a very important and personal case, involving messages from Ed Warren on the Other Side. The messages are perhaps the strangest chapter of all in John's long career in the paranormal.

14

Messages From Ed Warren

Our final chapter takes a turn into deeply personal material for John, involving the death of his uncle, Ed Warren, a heart attack, messages from Ed from the Other Side, and John's introspection about the meaning and direction of his own Work in the fields of demonology and the paranormal.

Rosemary here again in the first person, to tell this amazing story and the revelations that have taken place—and the mystery that still shrouds them.

The reckoning

On April 15, 2015, John Zaffis pressed his face up against the windowpane to the Other Side and then came back. Life has not been the same since.

When Johnny is at home, he spends a lot of time in his office in the barn, which also houses his Museum of the Paranormal. He always keeps a pot of coffee going in the main house. His wife, Cher, works during the day at a big corporation nearby. Her mornings are usually busy, and so John and she rarely talk by phone until late in the afternoon. Around five, John gets dinner going.

This day was different.

For John, the morning started out "strange." He could not shake the feeling that something was "off." He pushed it all aside and jumped into his work day. His hit reality television series, *Haunted Collector*, had recently ended after three successful seasons. He did not have the exhausting rigors of road travel and shooting, but he was still as busy as ever. Every day, there was a mountain of email, numerous phone calls, and cases to handle or initiate.

When the mail was delivered, John walked down his long driveway to fetch it, and then grabbed another mug of coffee in the kitchen before heading to his office. The office barn is in the back of the house, accessed by a small bridge connected to the deck.

John was halfway through the living room when suddenly he felt like hands grabbed him from behind and started squeezing his chest with tremendous force. Choking, he collapsed on the floor. Everything went hazy.

Abruptly the phone by the sofa rang, and John somehow was able to grab it. He was not near the phone when he collapsed, but now oddly, he was close enough to reach it.

Amazingly, it was Cher, making an uncharacteristic call home much earlier than usual.

"Come home, come home!" John gasped.

Cher slammed down the phone and raced out.

She was home in minutes, but for John, lying on the floor and hanging on to life, it was an eternity. All he could think about was, *Oh my God, I can't leave this mess for her and the kids to clean up... the museum... taking care of the business... they won't know where to begin.*

When Cher reached John, she wanted to call 911 for an ambulance. A hospital was nearby.

John refused. "I'm not paying five hundred dollars to drive one mile up the hill," he said in his stubborn way.

Cher helped John into her car and drove him to the emergency room. A kaleidoscope of bizarre thoughts and emotions swirled through him as the medical team rushed around. *Ma, if you're there, touch me,*

John thought, reaching out to his mother, Babette, who had passed away years earlier.

Doctors determined that John had a ninety percent blockage in one of his heart's arteries. He was stabilized and placed in intensive care while doctors planned surgery.

While John rested, conscious and hooked up to monitors, Cher kept a vigil in his room.

Word spread quickly that the star of *Haunted Collector* had been admitted to the hospital. People came in to see him and talk to him. Amazingly, one of them wanted to show him a video of an alleged ghost.

Cher objected. The man apologized and started to leave, and then said, "Can I at least ask what it was?"

John replied, "Dude, I don't know—there's something paranormal going on, I don't know what to tell you."

"This is too much," said Cher, getting up out of her chair. That was the end of the intrusions.

As she kept John company, Cher became aware of other visitors in the room—people who were not living. "Your mother, your father, your uncle—everybody is showing up in here," she said. "They're letting it be known that they are here."

John was taken aback. Were they present to usher him into the afterlife? Was this it? He closed his eyes. Everything was out of his hands.

Early that evening, doctors decided to operate on John and insert a stent. Cher had gone home for a while, and he asked the staff to call her.

In the morning before the surgery, the phone in his room rang—it was his older sister, Julie. Julie and John had had a family spat and falling out several years earlier and had not spoken to one another since then. Now she was sobbing on the phone.

"I can't let you die, let things end like this," Julie cried. "You'll be all right, the surgery will be good."

John asked Julie how she knew he was in the hospital facing surgery.

"Grandma and Mommy came and told me," Julie said, referring to deceased family members.

John and Julie cried together on the phone.

The family members from the Other Side did not come to help usher John out of this world, but to stand by with reassurances. John's surgery was successful, and he soon went home to recuperate.

Cheryl and paranormal investigator and *Ghost Hunters* star Dustin Pari put word out on social media about John's collapse, and fans reached out from all over the world with concern and prayers.

John was fifty-eight when he had his heart attack, the same age as his uncle, Ed Warren, when Ed suffered a heart attack and collapsed, about two weeks earlier in time frame than John. The significance was not lost on John. After his recovery, John pulled back from his paranormal investigations and work. It was time for a reevaluation of everything.

I asked John, "Did you have a classic near-death experience?"

"No," said John. "I joke around about it. I didn't see the pearly gates or the fluffy cloud. What I still can't figure out is why Cher called me so early in the day and right at that critical moment—she must have had an inner warning. I also can't figure out how I got near the phone to grab it. I was halfway through the living room when I collapsed."

Strange, indeed.

John emerged quite changed from his close call with eternity. He now has regular visitors from the Other Side: family members and close friends, who come with cryptic messages. The biggest and most frequent visitor of all is his uncle, Ed Warren. At least fifty witnesses have heard Ed deliver messages for John over their equipment during investigations, and some of John's mediumistic friends have had personal visits from Ed as well.

Why does Ed feel an urgency to pierce the Veil with continuing messages? In the months that followed, an even stranger story unfolded.

Ed Warren

Ed Warren was born in Bridgeport, Connecticut, on September 7, 1926. Warren was his middle name—his last name was Miney. His father was a state trooper and a devout Catholic, and enrolled Ed in parochial school. The Warren family lived in a big, old house rented out by a spinster landlady who did not approve of dogs or children, always throwing things at them in annoyance. Ed was five when the landlady passed away, and he saw his first apparition when she materialized in his bedroom closet a few days later, as sour as she had been in life. His father always told Ed that there must be a logical explanation for the paranormal behavior his son experienced, but never produced one. Young Ed would choose to stay outside in freezing or rainy weather rather than be in the house alone. One of Ed's supernatural visitors was a deceased woman. Ed had expressed a desire to become a priest, but the woman told him that he would not achieve that. Rather, he would consult with priests, and would do more work than a hundred of them.

When Ed was twelve, his family moved out of their haunted home. Although he had come to terms with the spirits there, his exposure to the paranormal just fueled his desire for more investigation and confrontation.

In 1943, when Ed was sixteen, he met Lorraine Rita Moran, also a native of Bridgeport. Ed enlisted in the U.S. Navy and served with the armed Navy guard aboard a Merchant Marine vessel that was attacked and sank. He was one of the few survivors. In 1945, while he was on leave, he and Lorraine married. They had a daughter, Judy.

After he was discharged from the Navy, Ed attended the Perry Art School, affiliated with Yale University. He left school to travel around New England painting landscapes and selling his oil paintings, and searching for haunted houses, his fascination. Ed would find haunted houses in a community, paint portraits of the homes, and give them to the owners. In return, he was often invited inside and was allowed to look around. Sometimes he and Lorraine became involved in counseling the occupants about paranormal problems.

Eventually, the couple's experiences as ghost hunters, and the wealth of information they collected, led the Warrens to the full-time pursuit of paranormal consultation, advising people on how to solve problem hauntings. In 1952, they co-founded the New England Society for Psychic Research. They became involved in some high-profile cases that received a great deal of media attention, such as the Amityville haunting—for which they served as consultants on the first film, *The Amityville Horror*—and built their reputation and fame. Ed and Lorraine were popular speakers, especially on college campuses. Working with writers, they published books about their best cases. They investigated abroad as well as throughout America, and were quite popular in the United Kingdom, Australia, and Japan.

Ed and Lorraine worked well as a team. After an invitation to investigate a site, they arranged a visit as quickly as possible. Once at the site, they usually split up. Ed conducted interviews of all persons involved, and Lorraine walked the property and home and used her psychic ability to discern spirit activity.

Over the course of fifty years, the Warrens handled more than 8,000 cases, according to their estimates. They amassed an unparalleled archive that included detailed interviews and reports from afflicted families and from other investigators; photographs; audio and video recordings of paranormal activity, including the voices of the spirits; a museum of spirit-attached clothing, dolls and other objects; and letters of gratitude from government officials, clergy and others. Several films have been made based on their work: *A Haunting in Connecticut*, about a haunted funeral parlor turned into a home; *Annabelle*, about a Raggedy Anne-type of doll haunted by the spirit of a little girl; *The Conjuring*, about a Rhode Island home they said was haunted by a witch, and *The Conjuring 2*, about the Enfield Poltergeist case in England.

The Warrens stressed that God does not let evil visit humans, but that humans must in some way invite the malevolence into their lives: by toying with the supernatural (conjuring, Ouija boards, séances, black witchcraft, and Satanic rituals); by sinking into negative, depressive states; or by obsession with a person or place. Ed referred to these "permissions" as the Law of Invitation and the Law of Attraction. Once allowed to enter, the demonic takes control in three stages: infestation, oppression, and possession. In severe circumstances, the final outcome could be death.

They did not perform exorcisms themselves, but worked with exorcists and assisted them. Ed and Lorraine strongly warned against anyone trying to perform exorcisms on their own.

Ed Warren suffered heart problems after a trip to Japan to assist in Buddhist exorcism techniques in 2001. On March 26, he got up at two in the morning to let in the cat and collapsed. Emergency crews were summoned, and it took fifteen minutes to revive him. Unfortunately, Ed suffered irreparable brain damage, and suffered severely impaired speech ability. He was hospitalized and was in a coma for several months. After convalescing in a nursing home, Ed returned to own home, where Lorraine cared for him.

It must have been unbelievably frustrating for a vocal man like Ed to lose his ability to talk well. He could shout and make noises, but had difficulty making himself understood. The last time John ever saw his uncle alive was in 2002.

Ed died on August 23, 2006, at age seventy-nine. He was buried with full military honors. Lorraine continues their work with family members.

Before his collapse, Ed was once asked if he feared death. He replied, "No, I don't fear it, not one iota, I know I'll be going to a beautiful place, a place so spectacular it defies words."

Ed and John

Ed was not the only person born on September 7, 1926 in the Warren household—he had a twin sister, Babette, or Babe for short. That woman was John Zaffis' mother. Research has revealed that twins often share telepathy, and Ed and Babe had their own bond.

While Ed pursued the paranormal, Babette was frightened of it, however, and did not want her own children involved in it. John, born on December 18, 1956 in Bridgeport, was the youngest of three children. He was psychically sensitive, and at a young age became fascinated by the stories Ed and Lorraine told about their cases.

When John was about fifteen, he had a bedside visit from an apparition. The transparent form of a man appeared at the foot of his bed, shaking its head as if to say "no." John's mother thought the apparition was his deceased grandfather. Shortly after the experience, his grandmother died. Had her husband come from the Other Side to let family members know in advance? It fits a pattern experienced by many others—early warnings via visitations and dreams.

Ed regarded John as a son and took him under his wing and mentored him, educating him about the paranormal, the demonic realm, and the pitfalls of dealing with the Dark Side—in other words, the "Work." Ed cautioned John that demons always try to destroy those who work in the field, and will, through temptation, try to make individuals destroy themselves.

John was determined to become involved, and Ed allowed him to actively participate in investigations when he turned eighteen. John spent about twelve years watching, observing, and learning, and then taking on more of a lead role.

The Scotland chapel St. Michael (Courtesy John Zaffis)

John accompanied Ed and Lorraine on a trip to the United Kingdom in 1988. He had a profound experience with the angelic realm, which prompted Ed to dispense valuable advice. Here is John's account.

> I was in a chapel in Scotland where I had my first encounter with the angelic in a way I never did before. I walked out of the chapel, and Ed was standing outside. He said, "What's up, kid?" He called me "kid" my whole life, no matter how old I was.

I told him that I had heard this piercing sound coming from all over in the interior of the chapel. It was so loud that I had to cover my ears.

Ed and I walked back into the chapel. He and I sat there for a few minutes and I looked at him and said, "What was that?"

His response was, "Angels." Ed then got up, looked up at a statue of St. Michael high on a wall, and said to me, "Pray and keep St. Michael by your side. You're going to need all the help you can get in this work, kid."

I looked up at St. Michael and took a photo. I sat quiet for the next few hours as we traveled to our next location. I was thinking about what had happened and Ed's words of wisdom.

John still has that photo of the Archangel St. Michael, and he has never forgotten Ed's advice. He keeps many statues of St. Michael in his office and home, and calls upon the services of Michael and other angels in his work, especially when dealing with the dark forces.

In 1998, John founded his own organization, the Paranormal Research Society of New England (PRSNE), and established a team to pursue investigations and cases.

John had strange experiences throughout his relationship with Ed, and not always involving cases—such as "the stained glass window":

I was very interested in finding the stained glass window my great-grandparents gave to St. John's Church in Bridgeport, Connecticut. As I was walking around the church snapping photos, I noticed that there was an old man sitting in one of the front pews. He seemed to be watching me as I was walking around taking pictures of all the windows. I passed by him and he asked me if I was looking for something in particular, or if I was just taking photos of things in the church. I told him that I was looking for a window that my great-grandparents had donated many years before.

He told me that perhaps he could help me, as he had been coming here for a long time. He then asked me if I knew anything about the window.

I told him all I knew was the family's name of Miney. He nodded his head as he told me that he knew many of them in that family. He then asked me if I was related to them. I replied that Frank Miney was my grandfather. Again he nodded and told me that he knew him well. I was surprised and happy to meet someone that knew my grandfather!

He then told me that the Miney window was in the staircase leading up to the balcony. Anxious to see it, I told him that I was going to go look at it but that I wanted to talk with him further if that was all right with him. Not saying anything to me, he lowered his head back down as if he was praying.

I went and took several photos. Then I headed back to the front of the church where he had been sitting, only to find out that he was now gone.

Disappointed that I could not finish talking with him, I headed back home. I began telling my mom the story of the window and the man that directed me to it.

My mom was curious and she asked me what his name was.

I told her that I had not gotten his name, as he was gone by the time I got back up to the front of the church. But I told her the funny thing was, he had on an old-fashioned straw hat, and that even though I knew that men always remove their hats before going inside a church, this man still wore his.

She just looked at me and told me to tell my uncle that story—my uncle, her twin brother, Ed Warren. Ed had changed his name from Warren Miney years before to his stage name of Ed Warren.

As I began telling him, he sat quietly just looking at me. Finally, he asked me what my mother had said about my experience with the man. I told him she had said nothing but that she had the same blank look that he had now on his face as I was telling my tale.

Not long after that day the church was closed and all the stained glass windows were sold off. I never knew what happened to the Miney window. As I reflect back on this story, even to this day, I never found out who the old man was, but somehow I think my mother and my uncle knew.

The church stained glass window (Courtesy John Zaffis)

Babette died in 1998. She made two after-death visits to John. The second visit occurred in 2004, just before John's father died. She made a bedroom visitation and stood by a dresser. After her death, Babette began appearing in Ed's dreams in advance of significant events in his life.

On an anniversary of hers and Ed's birthday, after Ed had died, John wrote this personal story:

> They say that there is a connection between twins, and that they share a lot of different things, and neither one of them is aware of it. Ed Warren and his twin sister, Babe, grew up in a haunted house in Bridgeport, Connecticut.

At the age of five, they had their first ghostly experience. They could hear someone walking up the front staircase into the kitchen and turn on the light, but no one would be there. This would scare them so much that they would hide in their bedroom under the bed. This would eventually lead Ed Warren into a career pursuing ghosts and haunted dwellings. His sister would not have anything to do with it, and if you asked her about the ghostly experiences, she would tell you to ask her brother Ed, because she was afraid of the supernatural.

Getting back to the connection between twins, Ed was not a psychic person, so for him to experience things with his deceased twin sister was something of a personal nature.

While Babe was in her home nearing the end, she experienced seeing apparitions of deceased family members. She would see her mother and several other relatives. I would ask her, "Mom, who is here in the room with you now?"

She would tell me who was with her. Then I would tease her and say, "Ask them how it is over there."

She would tell me that they would not say anything to her, they would just smile at her.

Then I would say to her, "How will I know what it's like over there when you cross over? You will have to come back and tell me."

My mother would get a serious look on her face, and wouldn't respond.

One day when I was teasing her about this, she looked at me, and said, "I'll tell you what, I'll come back and tell my brother that everything is okay over there."

I laughed and said, "Okay, Mom, you do that."

Several months later, she passed away. After her passing, I was visiting with Ed, and he came over and said to me, "I had a dream about my sister. I don't know if this is for you or your father, but she said everything is okay over there."

At that time, I remembered the remark she had made. At that point, every emotion inside of me went cold. I turned around and left the room. My emotions haven't been that wild since the day she died.

A short time after that I was with Ed, and he was telling me of the dream he had of his sister in a beautiful forest. In the forest he saw a lot of big trees, and a waterfall with her by it, and he said, "John, there were all kinds of beautiful flowers and all kinds of colors, pastels."

I asked, "What color stood out to you, Ed?"

"Why do you want to know that, John?" asked Ed.

"Just curious," I said.

"I think it was blue, some red, and pinks."

Stunned, I said, "Ed, blue was Babe's favorite color."

Ed asked me, "Why such an intense look on your face?"

I said, "I know I never told you or anyone else of a little remark your sister said to me, in regards to coming back, to let us know everything was okay."

Ed and I looked at each other and he said, "I guess now we know she is okay where she is."

And I said, "I'm glad she is in such a beautiful place."

I thought this story would be a nice tribute to the twins, and to know that it is true, you can communicate in different ways from beyond the grave. September 7th marks the birth of Ed and Babe, and unfortunately they are no longer with us. They were the two most guiding forces in my life.

Happy Birthday
Johnny

John's last conversation with Ed took place the day of his collapse in 2001. Ed's remarks foreshadowed his collapse, and also strange events that would not happen for more than a decade. John remembers:

It was March 26, 2001, a typical Sunday. I had headed up to the Warrens' to give them the weekly emails that

I monitored and to go over some of them with Lorraine. I was also visiting to review some of the cases I was working on for the Warrens. I headed for the living room where Ed was sitting, and I sat on the couch. We began talking about a few cases we were working on.

At that time, Lorraine's sister had come in, and she was giving Lorraine a gift. Ed and I were getting into some heavy conversation about the intensity of the Work. He looked at me and said, "Kid, you have to understand that I will not always be around. You have to start to make some decisions on your own with cases and stand on your own two feet. I know you have it in you to do that. I've seen you handle some very heavy cases and work with the researchers, helping them to understand this work. You know what to do, John."

I looked at him and said, "Why are you talking like that? You are perfectly fine and you will be around for a long time."

He put his head back in the chair, closed his eyes, and said to me, "I will always be around you one way or another. Just remember that and they will come at you from all directions. Just think back on what I would do, okay, kid?"

I was confused as to why he was suddenly talking to me about these things.

Just at that time, Judy and Charlie came in and Judy was upset over just losing her pet. They just stopped in to say hello. They saw my car in the driveway. Lorraine came in to see if we would like coffee, and went back into the kitchen to make some.

I looked back over at Ed and said, "Why are you being so serious about not being around?"

He opened up his eyes and smiled at me and totally changed the subject.

Little did I know that it would be our last conversation. He collapsed that night and went into a coma for several weeks. He finally came out of the coma, but with very limited abilities. In 2006, Ed passed away.

the box was located, or why the papers were important. The box remained a mystery, for Ed's repeated messages were *box... papers... listen... listen*, and the repetition of his name as well.

Ghost box and EchoVox messages

Ed soon spread his messages around to others who were in a position to relay them to John. He even enlisted the help of a few other discarnate souls to hammer away at John with messages, many of them repetitive. The majority of them have been conveyed through paranormal investigation equipment, devices known variously as the ghost box, Spirit Box, EchoVox, Frank's Box, Shack Hack, Minibox, and other names. These are all devices or apps that use sound for spirits and the dead to form words for real-time communication.

The most popular devices, such as the ghost box and Spirit Box, use radio sweep to rapidly scan the AM or FM band. In theory, this produces a jumble of sound that enables spirit voices to manifest. The mystery voices may speak words, phrases, or short sentences. These communications sometime seem to be formed by random but synchronistic words and phrases that pop out over the airwaves and are captured by the device, or else the voices seem to "ride" independently on top of the scan. Researchers ask questions and then wait for answers to be spoken on the devices. Sometimes the answers are given in real-time, audible to witnesses, and other times the mystery voices are passive, that is, they are unheard to the ear but are impressed on a recording device and can be heard on playback.

Some devices, such as the EchoVox, created by Daniel Roberge of Maine, are apps made for smartphones. They are programmed with phonemes, the building blocks of words. Every word in English, as well as most words in other languages, can be formed from twenty-four consonant phonemes and twenty vowel phonemes. To create the phonemes for the EchoVox, an Edgar Allan Poe book was read by both a man and a woman, and the word were chopped down into single syllables. The phonemes are played randomly, and in theory, the discarnate can manipulate them to form words in answer to questions.

Audio devices such as these have been in use in Electronic Voice Phenomena (EVP) and Instrumental Transcommunication (ITC) research since the mid-twentieth century. (Prior to that, researchers often used magnetic tape players to ask questions and get responses for playback.) Researchers discovered that a background sound, such as white noise, running water, fans, and crowd babble, enhanced results.

The EVPs from these devices and apps are controversial, and studies have both validated them and debunked them. Skeptics contend that researchers fall prey to "audio paredolia," in which the mind interprets sound as a familiar pattern where none actually exists. Thus, multiple witnesses might all "hear" something different.

It is true that many EVPs are hard to discern. Some, however, are quite clear, and the voices themselves are recognizable. I have used a variety of audio communication devices in the course of investigating. I believe that it is possible to receive communications that cannot be explained naturally. Such results have been well documented over the course of time, and a deeper discussion of this avenue of research can be found in my book *Talking to the Dead*, co-authored with George Noory.

What's more, devices do not work uniformly for all users. Some individuals get consistent and unusual results whenever and wherever they use the devices or apps. It is my theory that these people have a developed or latent psychic ability that is magnified by the device—they have an "affinity" with the tool that enables phenomena to manifest more readily. The sweep and phoneme devices are neutral tools, but in psychic work, tools facilitate the openings to the spirit realms. I have experienced this myself on many occasions, and I have also witnessed it on many more. Individuals who do regular work in the paranormal and with the spirit realms all have their own favorite tools, the devices or techniques that work the best for them.

John, who has had a natural sensitivity from childhood, has always gotten good results with audio devices such as the ghost box. Sometimes the results are increased when he works with others who are sensitive as well—a right mix of energies are formed.

Since John's heart attack, the ghost boxes and EchoVoxes have been chattering away. Not only has Ed come through, but others close to John as well—his parents, his sister, and Pat Reading and her daughter, Michelle (Pat Reading was a major demonic possession case, and both she and her daughter are now on the Other Side).

Carmen Reed, whom we met earlier in the demonic case of the Virgin Mary with the melted hands, was participating in an investigation at Poasttown Elementary School in Ohio in 2014 when she heard Ed, Pat, and Michelle speak in real time over the devices. All three voices were recognizable to Carmen, who had known them while living. "Ed's voice was very powerful and distinctive," Carmen said. "It was gravelly. He spoke like an Italian New Yorker. Ed always had a deep and commanding aura about him, and his voice represented that. I knew it was Ed—there was no doubt about it."

All three mentioned "notebooks," and Ed especially wanted to call John's attention to some unknown "notebooks." Ed also mentioned "papers." No one present, including John, knew exactly what Ed meant, and the sessions grew chaotic with too many voices chiming in.

Carmen's impression was that Ed was urgent about John understanding something about his work from a spiritual perspective, and about how things are presented to the public. "Ed has given me messages for John many times since his passing," Carmen said. "Usually I feel his presence more than actually hearing his voice. He asks me to tell John that he loves him, or that he needs to take care of something. He calls John 'kid' a lot. This time, he called him 'Johnny,' and that was different for me.

"Ed has always been protective of John," Carmen added. "He held him up as the son he never had. He is always around John."

Jenny Stewart is an investigator who has mediumistic ability, and has an affinity with ghost box devices and apps, for she gets extraordinary communication through them. Whenever she teams up with John, the communication goes off the charts.

Jenny never knew Ed in life, but she knows him well from the Other Side. Her first connection came during an investigation at Pythian Castle in Missouri. In a box session with Dustin Pari, the name "Andy" kept coming through. Neither knew who that might be. Later, Jenny was taking a break with John on the front porch and mentioned the mystery name.

"Oh my God, Jenny, I know who it is," said John. "It's Father Andy!"

Father Andrew Calder, who passed in 2012, was a popular figure in the paranormal and a good friend of John's. Andy was an ordained Episcopal priest with the Communion of Evangelical Episcopal Churches, and was also the founder of the Georgia Paranormal Research Team.

"What's Andy coming through the box for?" asked Jenny.

"I don't know, but come on, let's find out," answered John.

They started up the ghost box, and Andy came through about Ed.

"Is Ed here?" asked Jenny.

The response was a deeper voice. "Yes. I am here." It was Ed.

"What is your message for John?" asked Jenny.

"Pay attention to what's in front of you. You have to listen!"

After that experience, Ed came through a lot to Jenny. "That man is a chatterbox," she said. "I cannot do ghost box sessions now without Ed being around. First it was the ghost box, then it was the EchoVox."

The next time that Jenny and John were on the same investigation was an event at the Ohio State Reformatory in Mansfield. In group investigations, the celebrities are assigned stations to conduct EVP sessions for rotating groups of investigators. Jenny and John were stationed in the attic by the chapel. John was asking routine questions with a ghost box. Suddenly he shouted, "Oh God, no!" and lunged at Jenny. Fearing he was about to pass out, she thrust her hands out to catch him.

John recovered and managed to finish the rotation. After sending the other investigators on their way, he and Jenny lingered.

"John, what just happened?" Jenny asked, concerned.

"Ed just went right through me!" John exclaimed. "What does he want? He won't leave me alone!"

"He won't until you listen—he wants you to *listen*," Jenny said.

The Mansfield experience, Jenny told me, "shook us up pretty bad."

Jenny was also present at the Poasttown investigation and heard Ed come through:

"It's Ed… listen… Ed… Ed… listen…"

"Ed mentored John, and he is still mentoring him in death," Jenny said. "He's very proud of him and the work that he's doing. He thinks John does a great job. I think Ed is upset over the lies, misconceptions, and distortions of the truth that he sees out there in the field. John won't admit it, but the position and responsibility he has, I think it's overwhelming at times. There are times when decisions weigh on him a lot. He takes his work very, very seriously. Sometimes it becomes too much. He walks a path alone, we all know that. I think sometimes he feels very alone in the work that he does. Ed is always there for him."

Ed has mentioned "box" and "letters" to Jenny. She thought that perhaps "notebook" might refer to a note in a book, perhaps one of the books that Ed gave to John. Nothing significant was found. Ed, however, repeated that John has to "pay attention to what's in the book."

Is it a published book that John owns—or a book yet to be written?

Initially, John tried to ignore the communications, saying he was not ready to deal with them, but they persisted. "I think Ed needed me to give John a wakeup call," said Jenny.

Ed also started visiting Jenny at night to talk to her. Jenny knows instantly when Ed arrives. "I can feel him and I can tell," said she. "I don't know how to describe it. I know when he gets here. He sits down. There have been nights that I have been kept awake all night by him talking and repeating things." The communication is telepathic.

One night, Ed arrived and sat down on the edge of the bed. "You have to make him listen," he said to Jenny.

"I'm trying," Jenny responded.

"You're as hard-head as he is," Ed shot back.

"I can't force him," Jenny said.

Ed had a wicked sense of humor that he carried into the afterlife, and started delivering messages couched in riddles, which he repeated again and again. The riddles fell into Jenny's head whenever the whim apparently struck Ed, day or evening. They made no sense to Jenny, but they always did to John.

One of these riddle messages was delivered while Jenny was on an investigation at the Lizzie Borden House in Falls River, Massachusetts. The riddle was:

"*Three wise men were going up the river. One took a power boat, one took a paddle boat, one walked the bank alone. Who is the wiser of the three?*"

The answer was, the one who walked the bank alone.

When Jenny told John, he fell quiet. Then he said, "There's no way you would have known this…" He proceeded to relate how he had been in Mystic, Connecticut on the same weekend that Jenny was at the Lizzie Borden House. John had stopped in Mystic to get a bite to eat, and decided to take a walk along the river bank there. He mused about some buildings in town that might be potential places for his Museum of the Paranormal. A sea captain's old house was up for sale, and John wondered if Ed had ever investigated it, for it was reported to be haunted.

"I was standing by the water when you got this message," he told Jenny.

"He keeps telling me you should not fear walking the bridge."

John was silent for a moment. "I'm terrified of water," he responded. "When I was little, I was on a bridge that broke. My mom got to the edge, and my dad somehow held me by the hair to keep me from falling in."

Was Ed now John's constant guardian? Is John supposed to be a bridge in some way in his work, something that would put him out front alone? As Jenny observed, John walks alone on his path.

The riddle served only to deepen the mystery surrounding Ed.

The next riddle Jenny received was:

"Three wise men were at a party. One stood in a corner quietly and observed, one slipped away unnoticed, and the third sat in the middle of the room and became the center of attention. Who is the wiser of the three?"

John's response to this was, "Silence is golden," or, the one who sat quietly in the corner and observed. He is often fond of extolling the virtues of silence in his Facebook posts.

For Marc Arvilla, founder and lead investigator of the Mass Ghost Hunters Paranormal Society (MGHPS), hearing from Ed Warren was one of the last things he would have ever expected on an investigation. Once the communications started, Marc, his fiancée, Lauren Sheridan, MGHPS investigator, archaeologist and team researcher, and others found themselves front and center in the growing "Ed Mystery."

Marc tends toward the skeptical in the paranormal, and is a "show me" kind of investigator. For EVP, he often uses the EchoVox app, more for experimentation than for seeking hard evidence. The contact with Ed was a game changer.

Prior to talking to Marc, I spent a long afternoon with John reviewing EVPs from Ed during a session Marc conducted with the EchoVox app in Mystic, Connecticut, described later on. There was no doubt about it—Ed had made himself known.

The first time Ed came through to Marc was in 2014, well before John's heart attack, during an investigation in a private home in Beverly,

Massachusetts. The name "Ed" came through persistently, but no one knew who it was. Finally, a female voice came on and announced, "Ed, let's go," and the communications came to an end.

The mysterious Ed showed up again in a later investigation, but gave no further information beyond his name.

Houghton Mansion in North Adams, Massachusetts is a favorite of investigators, including the MGHPS. The former private residence, now a Masonic Temple, has intense hunting activity attributed to the original owners. There one night, Marc got the shock of his life.

He was conducting an EVP session in the temple when the mysterious "Ed" showed up once again.

"What is your full name, Ed?" Marc asked. "Are you trying to assist us with this investigation, or our other investigations? Why do you keep coming to us?" He repeated the questions. No answers.

Suddenly Marc saw a flash of a face in the darkness. It looked like a face that was lit from beneath by a flashlight. Illuminated were the chin, base of the top lip, beneath the nose, and a bit of the eyes.

It was Ed Warren! Even though Marc had never met the man, he had seen many photos of him, and his face was clearly recognizable.

This can't be possible, thought Marc. He ventured, "Ed, did I just see you?"

"Yes," responded a deep voice.

"Please tell me your last name."

"Ed Warren."

No way! Why is Ed Warren communicating with us? Marc wondered if somehow he was making it up.

Then he thought perhaps Ed had showed up to assist the team with their investigation. The link to Ed was broken again by the unknown female who showed up again. This personality had a harsh edge, and especially did not like Lauren jumping into the conversation. The unknown woman ordered Ed to leave, and both departed the session.

Afterwards, Marc thought perhaps Ed had a broader purpose of helping the living to communicate with the dead—but if so, why the MHGPS, and, more importantly, why were no other investigators in the paranormal getting the same treatment?

He reached out to John, someone he did not know personally, but in a professional capacity.

John told him, "You're not the first person who has told me something like this. You've described Ed's mannerisms to a T. Why is he talking to you?"

"I don't know," said Marc. "I was hoping *you* could tell *me.*"

After that, Ed was a regular drop-in on Marc's investigations. He would push other voices out and take control to get his own message through.

A breakthrough came in February 2016 when Marc and Lauren joined a few other investigators, including John, for a weekend in Gettysburg, Pennsylvania, another favorite hot spot in the paranormal community.

But when Ed came through, John was not receptive. "That's my friggin' uncle—what the hell does he want?" he grumped.

"I don't know," said Marc. "You're not listening."

"I don't know if I want to," said John.

But after more sessions where deceased relatives came through for some of the investigators in highly emotional sessions, John softened and asked Marc to set up the EchoVox for a private session.

Marc opened it with, "Okay, Ed, John is listening—what do you want to say?"

Ed gave his name.

"Who is with you?" Marc asked.

"Babe." That was the nickname of his twin sister, John's mother.

John jumped out of his chair. "You guys are blowing my mind!" He left the room in a hurry.

After a few minutes, John, now composed, returned.

The session revealed that John's great-grandfather was present, as well as other people whose names were meaningful to John. Ed repeated that John needed to take care of something and get some "papers."

"What papers? Who has the papers?" Marc asked.

Ed did not say. He then talked about the importance of a "box."

Despite the intriguing session, John was still not certain how involved he wanted to be.

Ed continued to intrude on Marc's sessions, and repeatedly talked about a "box," "papers," and "the book," all of which remained a mystery.

The next breakthrough came in the summer of 2016, when John asked Marc and Lauren to meet him in Mystic, Connecticut one Saturday afternoon. There, said Marc, they had "the most incredible session yet with Ed."

They started in a small cemetery, where they asked Ed what he wanted to convey, and he answered, "The box."

"What do you want us to do with the box," Marc said.

No answer.

Other names came out, among them "Paul," who apparently was a deceased person known to John, and "Steve." The session deteriorated into many voices, who then instructed the three to move to "the crypt" for better clarity. The "crypt" was probably a cold storage area at one time.

Paul dominated the resumed EchoVox session, and no more information was given about "the box."

The group was then told to go to the Old Mystic Inn. The proprietors were friends of John's. Even though this was a busy Saturday, luckily no one was in the main house but the owners. They all sat down in the breakfast room for the next session, and the owners joined them.

Ed identified himself. "It's Ed. You know. You know."

This time, Ed described the box as wooden, and answered affirmatively when asked if he had made the box. It was related to something extremely important to Ed, something John had to take and move his own work forward with it. Another name, "David," was given.

At one point, John said, "Ed, I don't know what you're trying to tell me, but every time I investigate, you're coming right through." In response, three louds bangs came right up through the floor, as though someone were pounding underneath the floor boards. Everyone jumped in their seats.

After that, the session flat-lined, and was brought to an end.

John explained that whenever Ed became frustrated while he was alive, he would bang his fist on a table.

But if Ed wanted people to understand his messages, he was not doing much to clarify them.

Throughout these experiences, Marc learned something personal about his connection to John. He once asked Ed, "Why me?" and was told, "Old soul." Apparently, Marc and John share an old soul bond.

Lauren has a great deal of psychic sensitivity. When the three of them get together—Marc, Lauren, and John—a "perfect storm" combination is created for EVP communications.

"There's something important here to Ed's work, and maybe all the work of future investigators," Marc said to me in retrospect. "Ed is coming through to more and more people who are connected to John. There are too many people and too much concentration on one subject. We're going to see something pretty amazing happen, sometime soon."

The circle widens

While working on this chapter, I discovered yet another Ed link, paranormal investigator David Weatherly. David lives in Arizona and is not a close personal friend of John's. Is he the mystery "David" mentioned in the Mystic sessions?

David conducts numerous investigators all over the United States and internationally, and uses a variety of devices, including ghost boxes known as Frank's Box, Geo Box, Shack Hack, the SB-7, and the SB-11, all of which have yielded up Ed—plus a Joe's Box that belonged to another investigator.

David met Ed and Lorraine Warren in the 1970s, when his budding interest in the paranormal drew him to them. They were two of a very small pool of researchers in the field, especially those who had attained fame. He never worked with them, but for a brief time, they were early role models.

Ed began intruding on David's investigations in May 2015, shortly after John suffered his heart attack. The first time the name "Ed" was given on an investigation, David—like Marc—thought it pertained to someone connected with the investigation site. But the name persisted at site after site. How many Eds could there be?

In June 2016, David was investigating various sites in Virginia City, Nevada, with a group. When he turned on the first ghost box, the name "Ed" name through immediately. It was drawn out, almost like a scream: *EEEEEEDDDDD... EEEEEEDDDD...*

David waited until everyone but one person whom he trusted had left the room, and then asked Ed for a last name. "Warren" came through loud and clear. At every site in Virginia City, on different devices, the full name "Ed Warren" came through.

Ed also delivered cryptic phrases. At the wedding chapel in the haunted Silver Queen Hotel, David asked Ed what he wanted them to do. "Follow the blood," came the answer.

Follow the blood? Did Ed mean his bloodline, John Zaffis?

Other terms were "legacy," repeated numerous times, and "take the crucifix." David had no idea what "take the crucifix" meant, but "legacy" seemed to refer to Ed's legacy, perhaps that which was being carried out through John. Ed also talked of "papers" and "files." He also said several times, "Help me."

Since the initial contact in May 2015, Ed has come through on almost all of David's investigations—just as he has overwhelmed the investigations of Marc and John. Ed sometimes starts off with, "David, are you there?"

"I think Ed is trying to communicate something to me," David said. "Whether it's a message for me or for John, or there are multiple layers to it, I don't know."

Dreams

Ed has even shown up in dreams concerning his messages. One of the most frequent ways that the dead communicate with the living is through visitation dreams. These are real experiences in a lucid bridge between the realm of the living and the afterlife—they are distinctly different from ordinary dreams. Most messages concern reassurance and closure, followed by unfinished business. Ed clearly has been pursuing unfinished business.

In addition to visitations, Jenny Stewart started receiving messages from, or concerning, Ed in her dreams. In one, she accurately saw Ed's former home office, a place she had never seen in person. That dream, she felt, was to demonstrate to John that she was indeed in touch with Ed in more ways than the ghost box.

Another dream was like a nesting box puzzle. In the dream, she saw Ed sitting in a leather chair with one tear running down his left cheek, and hundreds of red roses surrounding him.

At first, John did not know what the dream might mean. Then he received a phone call concerning an investigation case and an EVP recording that was not understandable to the investigators. Ed's name was presented, followed by the words "roses" and "sadness."

The tear down the left cheek may have been similar to Ed touching the left side of his nose to symbolize deceit. Was Ed sad over a deceit he saw in the field?

I was astonished to discover a dream visitation from Ed in my own dream diary from March 2010. In the dream, I was delivering a lecture on demonology in a large gymnasium. Ed was in the audience, sitting in the front row. I thought to myself that was interesting, because Ed was dead. He looked much younger and thinner than when he was alive. He stared at me with a neutral look. At one point, I stopped the lecture and engaged him in conversation. He mentioned two books, one with "letters" in the title and one with "files." I had the impression that the title of one of the books was *How to Be A Demonologist*.

As the dream went on, Ed continued to get thinner and younger.

I had no idea at the time that Ed was already conveying messages with those words—"books," "letters," and "files"—in communications to other people. I made no mention of it to John in 2010—it did not occur to me that there was any message in it for him. I forgot about the it. While working on this book, I discovered the dream while going through old files.

I had attended lectures given by Ed and Lorraine in the 1980s, but did not know Ed personally—so why did I receive this dream?

In my book *Dream Messages from the Afterlife* (2013), I discuss the characteristics and mechanisms of dream visitations. The energy behind these dreams is like electricity—it follows a path of receptivity. If the primary target cannot be reached—for whatever reason—then the dream goes to someone else who is in a position to get the message to the right person. "Dream proxy" visitations are quite common.

The fact that six years elapsed before I had an opportunity to relay the dream is meaningful as well. John was not ready to deal with the messages until 2015-2016. And for Ed, on the Other Side, time has no meaning, anyway.

I wondered about the dream book title, *How to Be A Demonologist*. The Warrens never wrote a book with that exact title, nor had John or I. I wondered if the title might pertain to John's work as a model or guide to others in the field.

David Weatherly has had dream visitations from Ed as well, reinforcing the messages of "follow the blood," asking for help, and telling David that he is present to help.

A penny from heaven

The genesis of this chapter took place in April 2016, when John and I got together at a diner near my home for a chat over lunch. As always, our conversation wandered over quite a bit of territory, and then suddenly John was talking about Ed and the messages.

Shortly after that turn in the conversation, two persons came into the diner and sat at the booth opposite ours. One was a Franciscan friar dressed in habit. We were astonished. There is a Franciscan Catholic church where I live, but in all the years I had been there, I had never seen a friar in habit in town.

We just shook our heads. Another sign from beyond! Pay attention! Listen!

John and I had a long talk about Ed and the messages. Finally, he said, "Whatever is going on... I don't know if I like this. I don't know if I'm comfortable in this environment with all these communications. The more I try to ignore him, the more tense things get. I've asked him point blank, 'What is it you want me to know?' and I still don't get an answer. It's gotten to the point where he shows up every time I investigate."

I fixed John with the most serious look I could muster. "There is only one thing for us to do here to get the answer," I said. "Get a Ouija board out!"

We both laughed. "You'll definitely hear from my uncle on that one, kiddo!" John said. Ed was famous for his opposition to the Ouija board.

"We've got a friar over there," I said, motioning to the man in the booth across from us. "We can ask him for help."

"I need several cardinals and the pope around me if this is ever going to happen," John quipped. He acknowledged that part of him did not want to know what Ed was trying to tell him. "When we go out of our comfort zone as investigators, and it hits too close and gets personal, I think all of us put that wall up," John said. "Do we really want to know? There are certain things we don't. I know that goes against everything we know as investigators, to learn everything we can to advance the field."

"If it were me, I'd want to know," I said. "Clearly, Ed is going to keep it up until this is resolved."

We parted company. I returned home. John, perhaps inspired by our conversation, decided to visit a holy place where he had found much refuge in the past: The Our Lady of Lourdes' Shrine in Litchfield, Connecticut. John had prayed there many a time when he was dealing with the Pat Reading demonic possession case, and he always paid a visit if he was in the vicinity. John took me there once on a beautiful fall day, after we had had lunch with Michelle Reading. It was the last time we saw Michelle alive, before her untimely death in 2012. The shrine is a pastoral setting, with an atmosphere of peace and serenity.

Shortly after I arrived at home, my cell phone rang. It was John, quite excited.

"Guess what just happened!" he said. He went on to explain how he'd decided to visit the shrine. "I went to the altar and lit a candle, and I was standing and praying, and suddenly a penny comes out of the air, flying right at me!"

"What!"

"It came right down from above, hit the candle and landed right on the ground," John said. "Ed used to say, 'A penny for your thoughts, kid.'" He paused. "I've never, ever, ever, *ever* had anything supernatural happen to me at the shrine."

"What did you do with the penny?"

"I left it on the altar," John said. "I said to myself, 'That's enough for me, I'm going home!'"

"John finally gets weirded out," I commented wryly. "Looks like our conversation about Ed ramped things up."

"This is getting to be a Sherlock Holmes kind of mystery," John said.

I agreed.

We end this book with the mystery still unsolved about messages about a box, papers, files, and a book or notebook, delivered with increasing intensity by a driven soul in the afterlife.

Listen! Pay attention!

We're listening, Ed—many of us now, not just a few. Tell us more.

The legacy continues.

Resources

More information on subjects in this book can be found in the following books and DVDs:

Books

Guiley, Rosemary Ellen. *The Encyclopedia of Ghosts and Spirits.* Third edition. New York: Facts On File, 2007.

_____. *The Encyclopedia of Demons & Demonology.* New York: Facts On File, 2009.

_____. *Guide to the Dark Side of the Paranormal.* New Milford, CT: Visionary Living, Inc., 2011.

_____. *The Djinn Connection: The Hidden Links Between Djinn, Shadow People, ETs, Nephilim, Archons, Reptilians and Other Entities.* New Milford, CT: Visionary Living, Inc., 2012.

_____. *Dream Messages from the Afterlife.* New Milford, CT: Visionary Living, Inc., 2013.

Warren, Ed and Lorraine, and Carmen Reed, Al Snedeker with Ray Garton. *In A Dark Place.* Graymalkin Media, 2014.

Zaffis, John and Brian McIntyre. *Shadows of the Dark.* iUniverse, Inc., 2004.

Zaffis, John and Rosemary Ellen Guiley. *Haunted by the Things You Love.* New Milford, CT: Visionary Living, Inc., 2014.

DVDs

John Zaffis: The World Within. DVD by Scared! Productions, 2010.

Websites

John Zaffis main website
www.johnzaffis.com

John Zaffis Museum of the Paranormal
www.johnzaffisparanormalmuseum.com

Paranormal Research Society of New England
www.prsne.com

Rosemary Ellen Guiley main website
www.visionaryliving.com

Djinn Universe
www.djinnuniverse.com

About the Authors

John Zaffis

John Zaffis is one of the best-known and most popular authorities in the paranormal. His career of more than forty years began with working with his uncle and aunt, Ed and Lorraine Warren, noted investigators and demonologists. John was drawn into paranormal investigation and demonology, and gained firsthand experience in cases of hauntings, possession, and exorcism. He has worked with prominent exorcists in Roman Catholic, Protestant, Jewish, and Buddhist faiths, among them Bishop Robert McKenna, Father Malachi Martin, and the Reverend Jun.

John's research has taken him throughout the United States, Canada, England, and Scotland. Over the years he has handled thousands of cases involving ghosts, poltergeists, demonic and diabolical entities, and haunted objects. He has also worked extensively with mediums and psychics concerning the afterlife, spirit communication, near-death experiences, and past-life recall.

John has been featured in numerous documentaries, television shows, and films, among them the Discovery Channel's *A Haunting in Connecticut* and *Little Lost Souls*; NBC's *Unsolved Mysteries*, *Fox News Live*; *Piers Morgan Tonight*, *Ghost Hunters*, and *Ghost Adventures*. For three seasons, he starred in his own paranormal reality show about haunted objects, *Haunted Collector*, on Syfy. He was a producer of the show in its last season. The series was picked up for reprise by Destination America.

John Zaffis: The World Within, a documentary on his life and work, was released in 2010 by Scared! Productions.

John is featured in *The Encyclopedia of Demons and Demonology* by Rosemary Ellen Guiley, and in *Graveyards* and *In A Dark Place*, by Ed and Lorraine Warren and various co-authors. John's first book, his autobiographical *Shadows of the Dark*, co-written with Brian McIntyre, was released in 2004. He is co-author, with Rosemary Ellen Guiley, of *Haunted by the Things You Love*, about haunted objects in his case files.

In addition, John runs the Paranormal Research Society of New England, an investigation group he founded in 1998. He makes numerous appearances on radio and is always in demand as a presenter at paranormal conferences and at colleges and universities.

Over the years, John has collected thousands of haunted items in his casework. In 2004, he created the John Zaffis Museum of the Paranormal to house the collection. John scripted and starred in a documentary film *Museum of the Paranormal*, released in 2010 by New Gravity Media, which gives a tour of the museum and highlights some of the haunted objects.

Websites:
www.johnzaffisparanormalmuseum.com and **www.prsne.com.**

Rosemary Ellen Guiley

Rosemary Ellen Guiley is a leading expert in the paranormal and metaphysical fields, with more than sixty books published on a wide range of topics, including nine single-volume encyclopedias. She has worked full-time in the field since 1983, researching, investigating, writing, presenting, and teaching. Her work focuses on problem hauntings; interdimensional entity and spirit contact experiences of all kinds; "portals" or geographic areas of intense paranormal activity; technological and mediumistic communications with the dead and spirits; the afterlife; angels; faeries; dreams; spiritual growth and development; and psychic skill building. She has done ground-breaking research on shadow people and the Djinn. She is also involved in ufology, cryptozoology, past-life regression, and reincarnation. She spends a great deal of her time out in the field conducting investigations and research.

In the metaphysical field, Rosemary has studied several modalities of energy healing. She is a certified hypnotist through the International Hypnosis Federation, and conducts past-life regressions. She also does lay dreamwork facilitation, and is a Tarot reader.

Rosemary heads her own multi-media publishing company, Visionary Living, Inc., and produces an e-newsletter, *Strange Dimensions*. She hosts a weekly radio show by the same name, *Strange Dimensions*, on the KGRA digital broadcast network.

She makes numerous radio appearances, and is a frequent guest on *Coast to Coast AM* with George Noory, She is featured in many documentaries and docu-dramas on the History, A&E, Syfy, Discovery, Animal Planet, Destination America, and Travel channels. She had two guest expert appearances on John Zaffis's *Haunted Collector*. In addition, she is a popular speaker at conferences, colleges, and universities.

Rosemary is an editor of *FATE* magazine, and serves on the board of directors and the research committee of the Dr. Edgar Mitchell Foundation for Research into Extraterrestrial Encounters (FREE). She is also a board director of the National Museum of Mysteries and Research, a nonprofit educational organization in Columbia, Pennsylvania. She is a former board trustee, and the present book review editor, of the Academy for Spiritual and Consciousness Studies, and is a founding member of the Afterlife Research and Education Institute.

In the past she served on the board of directors of the International Association for the Study of Dreams.

Websites:
www.visionaryliving.com and www.djinnuniverse.com.

17435807R00123

Printed in Great Britain
by Amazon